A Pen Named Man

A Pen Named Man

Our Destiny

JOHN W. NEWTON

RESOURCE *Publications* • Eugene, Oregon

A PEN NAMED MAN
Our Destiny

Copyright © 2013 John W. Newton. All rights reserved. Except for brief quotations in critical publications or reviews, no part of this book may be reproduced in any manner without prior written permission from the publisher. Write: Permissions, Wipf and Stock Publishers, 199 W. 8th Ave., Suite 3, Eugene, OR 97401.

Resource Publications
An Imprint of Wipf and Stock Publishers
199 W. 8th Ave., Suite 3
Eugene, OR 97401
www.wipfandstock.com

ISBN 13: 978-1-62564-006-2

Manufactured in the U.S.A.

All scripture quotations, unless otherwise indicated, are taken from the Holy Bible, New International Version®, NIV®. Copyright ©1973, 1978, 1984 by Biblica, Inc.™ Used by permission of Zondervan. All rights reserved worldwide.

Sharon L. Newton

A Pen Named Man: Our Destiny is dedicated to my wife, Sharon.

She is an exceptional human being who has made my life complete. Sharon has given unconditional love, respect, and commitment in raising our three children, Tim, Kim, and Rob, as well as our eight grandchildren, and seven other youngsters for whom she provided child care.

She has given her time and her love. She's played games, read stories, baked cookies, and made grilled cheese sandwiches. Sharon treated each child with respect in an uncompromising desire to have every one of them feel important and necessary.

Through it all, Sharon has taken care of our home and given me her love and unending support. She has also been an unselfish confidante and inspirer to our friends and other family members.

I love Sharon with all my heart.

Contents

Preface ix
Acknowledgments xi
Introduction xiii

1. Purpose and Essence 1
2. Societies and Institutions 5
3. Family 21
4. Religion 26
5. Government 43
6. Social-Economic: Employment 68
7. Health, Education, Recreation 102
8. Requisite Institutions 129
9. Evolution of Culture 141
10. Perspective 158

Bibliography 171

Preface

*God composes History on a music sheet called Existence
using a keyboard named Man with lyrics and notes known as Life.*

Acknowledgments

I WISH TO ACKNOWLEDGE our three children, Tim, Kim, and Rob. I'm so proud of each of them. Each one is unique in so many ways. Each has a distinct personality, yet all are identical when it comes to their dedication, love, and care for family and friends. They're exceptional human beings who are truly special to my wife, Sharon, and me.

Each has a wonderful family for which we are most happy. The greatest accomplishment we've been able to achieve is to marry and give life to children, who in turn got married and gave life to our grandchildren. Each one takes his or her special place in the world, and thereby is able to experience all the joys and happiness of living a highly meaningful life.

The best words ever spoken occur when I hear someone I love say, "Dad" or "Grampa". Family is life and family is love, and I'm so fortunate to have both.

God bless my family.

Introduction

As reported in *A Pen Named Man: Our Essence*, people have identical body systems. They share the same psychological functions as well. People have the same wants and needs. They have the same interests and develop similar attitudes in life. Further, there's a commonality of character which is evident in the realm of human value. Indeed, man's value system hasn't changed significantly for many centuries.

Thousands of years ago people cherished many of the values we believe in today. As example, consider the Golden Age of Greece. Several thousand years ago the human value structure was tied to a basic central theme. To the Greeks that theme was the "golden mean". The Greeks felt that everyone ought to eliminate extreme forms of behavior in his or her life. A person should seek and maintain a well-balanced position and accept the "golden mean" as the path to a rewarding life. Living in harmony with Nature was a worthwhile goal and that's the way a Greek citizen sought happiness.

Another example is illustrated by the citizens of the Roman Empire. At that period in history, people's values were likewise bound to a common belief. The Romans believed strongly in the role of justice across society. The Romans were committed to the rule of law. What was fair and right was what people sought, and it was supposed to be defined in law. Both the Greeks and Romans were successful in the structured approach they took to social living. Both were able to establish and maintain strong social systems based on a commitment to the common values of man.

The Roman orator, Cicero, acknowledged a number of common values that are universally held by mankind. Cicero stated, "The similarity of the human race is clearly marked in its evil tendencies as well as its goodness. For pleasure also attracts all men; . . ."[1] "But what nation does not love courtesy, kindliness, gratitude, and remembrance of favours bestowed? What people does not hate and despise the haughty, the wicked, the cruel, and the ungrateful? Inasmuch as these considerations prove to

---

1. Sprague, E. and P. W. Taylor, *Knowledge and Value*, p. 607.

us that the whole human race is bound together in unity, it follows, finally, that knowledge of the principles of right living is what makes men better."[2]

Today, the people of the world continue to support these common values. We all want justice. We want protection from the criminal elements in society and we want appropriate punishment for those who abridge the freedoms of others. Further, we all want certain rights guaranteed to us. For example, we want the right to vote, to own property, and to practice the religious teachings of our choice. Also, we all want equal opportunity within society. We want the opportunity to an education and the freedom to pursue a career of our choosing. In the arena of human values, people everywhere recognize the importance of truth, justice, and honesty. We appreciate the fact that compassion and concern are desirable human traits. We still are united against the evils of tyranny and we disapprove of coercion and oppression. Furthermore, we condemn crime. We deplore violence which harms people in society. We still care about our fellow citizens and we seek to support those people in need. We all enjoy beauty. We all wish for love.

People's lives are affected by biological influences like heredity and cultural factors such as social environment. Indeed, we are a product of our whole biological-cultural evolution. As a product of our times, we live according to the way we are taught. If we're taught to live by strict rules we do so, and if we're taught to live free and unbound we behave accordingly.

In general, we adhere to current social values and do what's expected of us. That is, we follow the sanctioned laws of the land. We don't physically harm other people. Nor do we steal. When we drive our cars we stop at traffic signals. We likewise adhere to the unwritten rules of society. For instance, we do not cry in public. And when waiting in line to purchase tickets to a movie or sports event, we don't crowd ahead. Additionally, we function in a manner to win the acceptance of others. That is, we're polite and show respect to our elders. We also try to help the people in need.

A characteristic of human beings everywhere is the desire to be secure. We all seek stability in life and that's a major reason why people established elaborate social structures in the first place. Within a social system we maintain a police force. We provide and maintain a militia as well. Coincidental with installing physical security is the attempt by people to institute sound economic systems. We want businesses and industries in place which will serve as stable and productive places of employment.

2. Ibid.

We want educational facilities that are of benefit to our children as well. We also want a guaranteed system of health care. Overall, people seek a secure life that's free from uncertainty and hardship. Overall, we wish to be happy. Our possessions such as our homes are very important to us. Further, an allegiance to our nation and its government is important. Our entire cultural heritage is of value and we feel we have a meaningful place in the world. Thus, we feel we have a contribution to make to society. Because of this, we are inherently confident about our place in the world.

What's important to the human species relative to its future, hundreds and even thousands of years from now? Where is the species of man headed and how does it get there? A logical progression to our cultural development suggests the establishment of a universally-based social-economic system. A universal social-economic system would provide every employed person with the basic necessities of life. In return, the individual would work in an occupation directed towards the betterment of mankind. The employment structure needs to be designed so an individual can attain pride and satisfaction in his work, and society as a whole benefits from the labor the person performs. It must be structured so a person doesn't enter an occupation for reasons of fame, power, or financial wealth. Rather, one enters a profession for the reward of personal fulfillment. The employment structure must be designed so the individual is able to meet one's purpose in life through his or her accomplishments on the job.

In this book we examine the culture of mankind and identify the major institutions of society. Each institution's role is to ensure progress in key areas of social living. The institutions range from family to government to religion. They further range from employment to education to health care. We see how they exist today and project how they might be structured in the future. Finally, we discuss how the creation of universally-based social institutions might better meet the needs of man.

In proposing the formation of redesigned universal institutions of society, it's important to note we use the term "universal" in two different, but related contexts. One is the traditional definition, meaning it applies to the entire world with all its citizens. That is, a universal institution, such as government, religion, employment, education, health care, etc., is representative of a world order in which there's a single society of people across the planet. It's based on the assumption that one day the world will be comprised of a single constituency, derived and desired by the vast majority of the world's citizens. On Earth, everyone would live under a single jurisdiction should the institution be government, under a single set of spiritual beliefs should the institution be religion, and under a single socio-economic design should the institution be employment. The precepts and values held by any particular institution are defined in an all-encompassing manner. The institution's operating principles would be accepted and followed by every person regardless of the ethnic background, race, or geographical home to which he or she belongs.

The other definition is based on the premise that a universal institution pertains to a single set of operating principles within an individual nation, and collectively, all the nations share in these operating principles. The principles are modeled after the proposed components of a worldwide institution. It's like a United Nations of institutions that's set up for each major sphere of societal life such as government, religion, employment, education, etc. Every nation would share the same basic beliefs, values, principles, etc., except they're likely to be modified to some extent to accommodate the nation-by-nation distinctions that are typified by regional, ethnic, and racial differences or backgrounds.

Let's illustrate the differences between these two definitions by way of example. Relative to the first definition, there would be just one nation of citizens across the entire world and its "universal" religion would hold the belief that God is the creator and spiritual or moral authority of the universe. Regarding the second definition, for a collection of separate nations, each with its own variation of a "universal" religion, all of the religions would independently express a belief in God as the creator and moral authority of the universe. Hence, every major religion would share in that commonality. Another example would be the belief in the ultimate goodness of the human nature or soul. All major individual religions together, or only a single religion of the world, would hold this premise, i.e., that the ultimate goodness of mankind represents a fundamental religious principle. We list the basic beliefs and precepts that a universal religion would contain in chapter 4.

Similarly, for government, there would be one government that runs the entire world and it would be structured similarly to the way we describe in chapter 5. That is, it would have a legislative and executive branch to prepare and enact the laws of the land. It would maintain a police force to control the criminal elements of society, as well as a judicial system to hear disputes between the citizens or corporations. Relative to the individual nation model, it would consist of an assortment of governments throughout the world, all of which are structurally similar. Operation-wise, they'd maintain and uphold the fundamental precepts of equality and justice for all citizens regardless of sex, age, ethnic background, national origin, or economic status. Each government would house its own legislative and executive branches. Likewise, each would maintain its own police force to deal with crime, in addition to a court system to settle disputes between corporations or the citizens within its jurisdictions.

Relative to a universal socio-economic design, there would be either a single world-wide employment structure as we describe in chapter 6, or an association of several national socio-economic systems, all of which are similar in structure and operation. That is, each national socio-economic system would provide an employment structure whereby the citizens would work to manufacture a product or provide a service that's useful to the betterment of mankind. In return, they would earn the benefits to meet their primary needs of food, clothing, and housing, as well as other requirements for comprehensive health care, education, and so forth.

The application of either of these two definitions satisfies our intent in this book to define the overall scope of a universal institution of society.

1

Purpose and Essence

In *A Pen Named Man: Our Purpose* we discuss EXISTENCE-LIFE-GOD. EXISTENCE is the domain, LIFE is the substance, and GOD is the quality of being. We describe the Animate Form of Life as one major ramification of EXISTENCE. We further describe a major component of the Animate Form of Life which is the universe with its multitude of galaxies, stars, planets, and satellites. We continue our discussion of the universe by examining the Milky Way galaxy plus one of its solar systems, specifically the one containing our sun and planet Earth. Spaceship Earth is our home and the abode of animate life within the solar system.

We examine the here of being. We describe EXISTENCE as the realm where everything takes place. In addition, we investigate LIFE as the fundamental substance behind all reality. We go on to describe the major components of the universe including the living and non-living worlds. We describe the inanimate objects like hills, rocks, and streams, as well as animate beings including the numerous species of plant and animal life. We further discuss GOD as the third member of the EXISTENCE-LIFE-GOD triumvirate. GOD represents the quality of being and the very spirit or essence of Life.

In *A Pen Named Man: Our Essence* we examine a representative species of life within the Animate Form of Life. The one we examine is the human species. We note the fundamental essence of Life, GOD, gives rise to all species including mankind. GOD, as the "universal soul", gives rise to the human organism that contains both biological and non-biological components. We then describe the major body systems and discuss the life processes they carry on. We also discuss the psychological make-up of man. We describe the human mind and discuss how emotion and reason are used to control behavior.

We further investigate the driving forces behind these two major components. We note the physical and psychological realms have requirements of their own, and the requirements must be satisfied to ensure good physical and mental health. We describe how man's biological and non-biological components interact with one another. Furthermore, we demonstrate the need to synthesize them into a compatible and workable union.

We find the human being to be a unique and highly complex organism. From our studies, we know that across the spectrum of the Animate Form of Life, mankind is a worthy representative of all organisms to have life.

In both books we talk about the role of scientific discovery in the world. Without question, the role of science is important, since the application of scientific technology can alter the life of man. For instance, mankind can improve the performance of his physical body. The control of the body and its parts are in the hands of the physicians. The placement of artificial tissues and organs within the human body allows man to improve his physical structure and prolong life. Similarly, mankind can advance his emotional well-being. The control of the mind and its moods are in the hands of the psychologists. The administration of behavioral influencing drugs permits man to regulate his drives, feelings, and needs. Furthermore, genetic engineering is a reality. Research in hereditary science can direct the development of the human organism in both its physical and mental realms.

Advances in the areas of physical and mental health can improve the human station in life. Nevertheless, science will not satisfy all of man's needs. There are philosophical issues that arise and theological solutions that must be found. The human organism seeks a set of universal values to live by. Mankind wants a clear distinction between right and wrong. Man seeks a "complete" behavioral pattern based upon moral principles. He desires spiritual satisfaction in life and, for the most part, seeks it through involvement in the church.

We note man's universal quest to improve his station in life is through advances in social living. Some key elements to achieving this quest include the following. He must use reason to solve everyday problems. Likewise, he must pursue activities which will bring about community succcess as well as employ constructive work efforts in order to sustain economic prosperity. Further, he must be honest and remain dedicated to the values of fairness and justice. We also recognize mankind must continue to focus on maintaining a moral order in society. Additionally, he must strive to be outgoing and friendly; and finally, man must continue the pursuit of personal happiness.

Man desires a forward looking, more prosperous way of life as reflected in a standard of living that continues to rise. He desires a life style that's more enjoyable and rewarding. Indeed, he desires a daily routine which is easier, safer, and more comfortable. To attain these ends, mankind has become specialized in his occupational and social roles.

Until present time, mankind has only been able to meet the basic needs of survival. However, now he has time to spare. Due to more effective medicines and better nutrition, people enjoy healthier lives. They live longer. Likewise, people don't need to work twelve to sixteen hours a day just to provide food, clothing, and shelter for themselves. In addition, the level of education has advanced for every demographic group of society. Children are better educated. Adults receive better training on the job and are afforded a greater opportunity to succeed in the workplace. Overall, society has become considerably more efficient at producing basic goods and delivering needed services. This has left more time for people to pursue new interests in life.

Considering the extent of cultural evolution to date, there's considerable diversity among the billions of people who inhabit planet Earth. As we know, the people of the world vary in national allegiance. Some people prefer to reside in the country of Canada while others desire to live in Great Britain. Other people choose to be citizens of China, Japan, India, etc. As far as topographical regions are concerned, people differ as to where they wish to make their home. Some people want to live on mountain sides while others prefer to live on the flatlands and plains. Still others are content to live in the desert areas. People also vary in the form of government they support. Some people desire to live within a democratic system of government, whereas others are satisfied under a monarchial regime. People also vary in the type of religious doctrine they ascribe to. Some people belong to the Islam faith. Others ascribe to the religions of Judaism, Christianity, and so forth. People further vary in the languages they speak. Some people speak the Russian language and others speak English. Still other people speak French, Spanish, or Italian. People even vary in the way they eat their meals. Some people use knives and forks to eat with, some use chopsticks, and still others use their fingers. Human culture is as varied as the interests of its many members, and unquestionably, the world's population shows a wide variety of interests.

Mankind can progress. He can establish a culture with common goals. The people of the world can put in place the universal institutions of employment, educational, health care, and so forth. Hence, the continued advancement of the human race is the responsibility mankind has assumed; and the arena where he can implement this charge is through a redesigned social-economic system.

2

Societies and Institutions

OVER SEVEN BILLION HUMAN beings are now alive, which accounts for more than half the total number ever born. Altogether the world's population comprises several races and sub-races, scores of nationalities, and hundreds of ethnic groups. There are nearly two hundred separate nations in the world and collectively these nations exhibit a wide assortment of economic structures, religious orders, and systems of government. The nations vary in language and custom. They display a multitude of beliefs, values, and social norms.

The societal diversity we refer to is not a result of man's biological make-up. Physiologically, the human organism has remained the same for hundreds of thousands of years. The diversity is due to man's cultural development; and over its long history, the human species has built highly elaborate social structures.

As human culture spread across the earth, a number of social systems developed. The differences are seen in many areas, one of which is population size. Some societies are very large with several hundred million members, whereas others remain small with just a few thousand people. Societies further vary in time of duration. Some societies last but a few hundred years while others remain intact for thousands of years.

Societies vary in geographical location. Some social communities are located on mountain sides and some are settled in the valleys. Some societies are located along the seashore, whereas others are planted on islands. Societies vary in geographical area as well. Some cover millions of square miles and others are concentrated on a few thousand acres of land.

Societies vary in the predominant means of personal mobility. In all societies people travel by foot. The members of some social systems travel by boat as did the ancient Norsemen of Northern Europe. Others traveled by horseback as exemplified by the Plains Indians of North America. In modern societal systems, like the United States of America, the vast majority of people commute from home to work by automobile.

Social structures vary in complexity. That is, the societal fabric varies from tribal to industrial. Some societies have people living in tents; others have people living in clay and wooden shelters; and still others have people residing in concrete and steel buildings, i.e., hotels and high-rise apartments. Societies vary in economic design as well. Some societies are rural in nature wherein most people support themselves by working in agriculture. Within such a socio-economic scheme, the majority of families live on farms and in small towns. Others societies are industrially based. For these, the people are employed in manufacturing with a majority working in shops and factories. Industrial based societies have members employed in communication, transportation, and commerce. A large proportion of the families within this design are concentrated in cities and urban areas.

Societies vary in the approved system of law. Some societies are based upon a strong sense of law and order as typified by the Roman Empire of over 2000 years ago. At the other end of the spectrum are societies based upon barbarism. Those societies reflect an absence of law and order.

Societies vary in class structure and the roles that people assume. Some societies demand servitude from its various members. Such societies bind people physically as embodied by the caste systems of ancient Egypt and nineteenth century America. Such societies use slave labor to perform the most difficult of jobs. Other societies are structured on an unrestricted access to employment. They promote a system of free enterprise and utilize democratic principles as the basis for government. Twentieth century England, Canada, and France are examples of such countries that champion open markets and personal liberties. Still other social structures promise freedom and opportunity yet devise ways to bind people through "economic" chains.

Regardless of a society's final structure, there is a historical pattern to the way most societies develop and grow. Typically the family is the beginning point from which a social structure develops. The family grows in size, acquires livestock, and takes control of the surrounding land. The family takes in new members through marriage and becomes self-sufficient. It develops as a mini, socio-economic unit in its own right. One family begins to cooperate and trade services with another family; and at some point, the families within a select territorial region join together. Through a commonality of economic needs and social objectives, key allegiances are formed. With time a number of families band together to form hamlets, villages, and towns. Eventually, cities are formed. The people within a city divide the workload and take on problems which were once solved by an extended family. And through a sharing of responsibilities, the urban dwellers meet their needs in a more efficient manner. As time goes on the unification process flourishes. One by one the neighboring villages, towns, and cities join together into larger and more durable alliances. The desire for the extended social structure persists and eventually principalities and regional states are established. Ultimately this leads to the creation of a nation.

There are several significant reasons why people decide to establish societies. No doubt choice plays a key role. Mankind establishes societies because he wants to. A human being is comfortable with and likes being among other human beings. Indeed, for the most part a human being isn't a loner. He is born into a family and throughout his life he's in close contact with others.

Another major reason why people establish societies is because human needs are better met inside a social environment. This concept was aptly expressed by the seventeenth century philosopher John Locke. According to Locke, people are motivated to live and work together. They recognize there are more advantages to being together than being alone. People yield their independent status when they form a social organization and give up certain private rights in order to gain public rights, rights designed to promote a successful social-economic environment. Thus, the presumption is: human needs are more easily met when people face life's problems together. Therein lies the basis for Locke's "original compact" theory of social living.

A third significant reason to form a society is centered on the desire for self-preservation. Jean Jacques Rousseau was an eighteenth century philosopher who believed the safety issue was a fundamental reason why societies are formed. According to Rousseau, people come together to form social structures to achieve protection of self and property. The people who join an alliance vow not to fight with other members of the alliance. Once united, the people are inherently stronger against outside enemies. Rousseau further stated that every person receives certain rights and privileges; and as a member of society, each person is obligated to respect the rights and privileges of other members. For the most part, Rousseau's "social contract" theory states that the mutual support for one another's needs promotes a peaceful social environment.

A fourth major reason why people become members of a social environment is because they're forced to. Not everyone enters a new social structure on a voluntary basis. Rather, it's a question of participate or die. At times of war, for example, a more powerful political state attacks a less powerful state and defeats its people militarily. As a result, the defeated people are forced into a new social structure.

Social structures then are established for the above reasons. People are gregarious and enjoy living with others. They discover they can accomplish more and provide greater services by working together. People recognize protection is better afforded if united. And finally, societies are established because people are conquered and forced to live among their conquerors.

Regardless of the reasons to establish them, once established, the social structures meet the needs of man. Societies provide services which must be provided and solve problems that occur on a daily basis. Societies afford certain benefits to individuals which they cannot easily attain for themselves. Although it may be true that most human needs can be met by any person living alone in Nature, a return to Nature's scenario isn't attractive to the vast majority of people. That's because human needs are more effectively met when people work side-by-side in a social-economic environment.

Cultural progress illustrates the numerous advantages to living in a group environment. For example, by working together people can effectively meet their need to obtain food supplies. Working together, people can build farm machinery such as tractors and combines. They can plow the fields. They can plant seeds, spread fertilizers, and irrigate the soil. Together, they can gather the fruit from the fruit orchards and harvest the vegetables and grain crops. They can maintain huge dairy farms and operate the poultry, hog, and cattle ranches. By coordinating their efforts and distributing the work load, people can produce food effectively and on a large scale. Likewise, the food can be delivered through a vast transportation network to a variety of outlets including produce markets, corner delis, small grocery stores, and the large food chains.

Thus, the efficient production and distribution of food allows the majority of people to live away from the farms. People are able to live in towns and urban areas, and once there, they can work to satisfy the industrial needs of society. That is, they can design and make new tools. They can build motors, machines, and heavy-duty equipment. They can manufacture appliances for their homes. On factory lines they can assemble automobiles. And to satisfy their clothing needs, they can sew new garments and wearing apparel. Also, they can make shoes and other footwear in a highly productive fashion. Working together, people can erect office buildings and high-rise apartments. Likewise they can construct schools, libraries, and hospitals throughout their communities.

There are numerous benefits to concentrating the work force. As mentioned, the manufacture of goods is accelerated and the provision of services is greatly enhanced. Additionally, urban living facilitates the introduction of new advances in the fields of communication and transportation. And as the level of technology expands, industry progresses. Typically the net effect for all members of society is an increase in their standard of living.

In *A Pen Named Man: Our Essence* we list the various needs of mankind. We talk about the physiological requirements of the body. We discuss the several body systems and their requisites for biological survival. We also review the psychological demands associated with the mind. We talk about the inherent need for security and emotional stability, including man's desire to seek and attain happiness in life.

Since the human adventure unfolded on Earth hundreds of thousand of years ago, mankind has held these needs. Over time, mankind has devised an assortment of ways of meeting needs whether biologically or psychology based. Let's briefly review some basic human needs and the avenue man uses to effectively satisfy them.

Man requires food to survive so he finds ways to obtain food. He fishes in the streams and lakes. He hunts in the forest. He raises chickens and pigs, and he domesticates cattle and sheep. Man slaughters the livestock in order to eat. He plants vegetables in the garden and he harvests crops in the fields. In addition, man goes to the corner deli to shop. He attends the farmer's market to select fresh produce and he purchases groceries at the local supermarket. In every case, mankind procures food for himself.

Mankind seeks shelter for himself as well. He continually seeks protection from the rain, wind, and cold. Consequently, he builds homes to live in. Whether the person lives in a cave, a tent, a house, or an apartment building, he provides shelter from the elements of Nature.

Mankind has the need to educate his children. He trains his children in various methods of survival. He teaches them how to fish and hunt. He also shows them how to set animal traps in the woods. He teaches his children how to cultivate the soil and harvest crops. He teaches them how to use tools. He teaches them the skills of carpentry and how to install floors, wall partitions, and plasterboard in order to build a house. He also instructs them on maintaining a household, which includes how to prepare meals, do laundry, and sew clothing. In addition, man provides formal instructional schooling for his children. He sends them to elementary schools, high schools, and colleges. He sends his children to prep schools and trade schools as well. Man educates his children on how to function satisfactory in a modern, social-economic environment.

Man has the need for health care, hence he regularly seeks medical attention. The treatment a person seeks covers a broad spectrum ranging from first aid to hospitalization. First aid is the initial line of protection and is typically used for the treatment of minor cuts and bruises. Hospitalization is the most rigorous treatment option and it's used for the recovery from life-threatening illnesses. For instance, serious operations such as open-heart surgery and brain surgery are performed in the hospital. Hence, a person seeks the level of medical care which satisfies the seriousness of the aliment. Whether a person seeks out a paramedic, a nurse, an intern, a general practitioner, a specialist, or a surgeon, the individual is seeking care for a medical problem.

Man has the need to get along with his fellow man. Therefore, he diligently pursues social justice. He has the desire to safeguard property rights. He also has the desire to ensure the equitable transfer of goods and services. Man further has the duty to maintain law and order throughout society, and pursuant with that responsibility, is the requirement to apprehend and punish those individuals who violate other people's rights. Government is the institution established to meet these objectives. And whether one lives in a monarchy, a totalitarian state, or a democracy, a person lives under a political system that functions to maintain order in society.

Mankind has the need for emotional security. He continually seeks moral and spiritual guidance in life. A person's psychological well-being is founded in a belief of the divine, and no matter what one's religious convictions are, a person seeks divine inspiration. The institution of the church is designed to help man fulfill his spiritual needs. Hence, houses of worship are established across society. Whether a person practices the religion of Buddhism, Hinduism, Confucianism, Taoism, Islamism, Judaism, or Christianity, he seeks moral direction in life.

Mankind has a need for philosophical enlightenment as well. He always seeks awareness and understanding. He expresses awe in the vastness of the universe. Man feels that some force or power much greater than he created the universe. Man seeks to identify the source of this power and whether one identifies the source as a distant planet, the sun, the moon, a universal soul, or God, he recognizes there's a creative force behind all reality.

The needs and problems of society are the same needs and problems of an individual person. Indeed, society is comprised as the collection of individual people. What a person wants is what society wants and what a person needs is what society needs. Society's needs and problems, however, are more broadly based. Society's needs require the provision of goods and services for hundreds of thousands, even millions of people.

An established social structure can solve problems in a more expedient manner than individual people can. A well-designed, social-economic system has the overall benefit of saving labor and time. It provides for the manufacture and distribution of products on a broad and rapid scale. It also allows for meeting the service needs of everyday life in a highly efficient manner.

To adequately meet the needs of its people, a society has several important functions to perform. Some of the main duties a society is charged with include the following.

People within a society must establish the framework by which the economy operates and further determine how responsibilities are delegated across key functional groups. For instance, people have to determine how the food is produced. They must answer questions such as: Where will the grain crops be planted and reaped? Will there be fruit orchards to harvest? Will there be poultry and dairy farms? Will there be cattle ranches and other large agricultural complexes? The people also have to determine how the goods are manufactured and distributed. Will the products be mass produced in factories in assembly-line fashion? Likewise, people in society have to determine the division of labor. Will there be open and direct employment for everyone? Will it be a co-operative or collective-type system of employment? Or, will some form of indenture service or slave labor be used to achieve productivity ends? People have to further determine how power is supplied. Will coal and oil be the major sources of energy, or will nuclear power plants fulfill most of a nation's energy needs? The people in society also have to determine how materials are delivered. Will there be vast highway and railroad networks in place? And how will the trucking, shipping, and airfreight systems operate? Further, people have to determine how communication occurs as well. Will nationwide telegraph and telephone systems be installed? Additionally, will radio and television stations be established throughout the country?

People within society must ensure their personal well-being is provided for. A society has to be structured so homes and apartment buildings are built and maintained. Also, people have to determine where their children are educated. Accordingly, a society establishes both public and private school systems. Additionally, people must determine the means whereby the elderly are cared for. Consequently, nursing facilities and homes for senior citizens are constructed. Further, people must ensure that an appropriate health care system is in place. As a result, society provides dental clinics and medical centers. It also builds hospitals where the ill can be treated and cured.

People within a society have to define the various roles of key components of its infrastructure. Employment positions need to be decided. Hence, the roles of the policeman, teacher, doctor, lawyer, etc., are determined. Likewise, the roles of the farmer, factory worker, shoemaker, shopkeeper, etc., are defined. Peer groups, work groups, and business associations need to be characterized. Furthermore, for a society to be successful, the employment structure must be sound. The socio-economic system must be stable and provide the opportunity for all citizens to earn an adequate living.

People within a society must identify and sanction proper moral behavior. Parental responsibilities, as well as church and state duties, must be resolved. Thus, the codes for appropriate behavior are written and the rules of good conduct are legitimatized. Thereby, people within a society establish the day-to-day operational norms.

People have to ensure their social structure survives. To do this, a society installs the mechanism to meet the legal requirements of its people. It sees that personal rights are guaranteed and a system of government is in place to draw up, ratify, and enforce the laws. Additionally, the people need to make sure internal peace is maintained. To do this, a society establishes a police force in order to maintain law and order. Hence, it establishes a system of civil and criminal courts as well as rehabilitation facilities such as reformatories, jails, and prisons to deal with criminals. Finally, people in society must ensure that peace is maintained with foreign nations.

Consequently, each state maintains a military presence by equipping itself with an army, navy, and air force.

Every society is structured to satisfy the functions and requirements identified above. Every society is organized such that the responsibilities to accomplish those functions are divided among the major internal units we call institutions. Institutions help people meet their needs and solve problems which confront them on a daily basis. In addition, they provide a sense of stability to established practices associated with the home, workplace, school, church, etc. Institutions help preserve the type of life that people deem important and reinforce the permanency of "good and decent" social living.

The major institutions of society include the following. Without question, the most important institution of social life is that of family. Besides family, there are the major institutions of government, religion, and employment. Also, there are the key institutions of education, health care, and recreation. Additionally, there are the institutions of communications, transportation, and financial resource. Finally, there are the institutions of utilities-services, energy, ecology, environment, and discovery.

Some social institutions such as the institution of religion are well organized. The institution of religion, for example, is rich in tradition and has an extensive operational protocol built on pageantry and ceremony. The institution of the church is representative of an elaborate ecclesiastical hierarchy that's developed over many centuries. And during that time, the church has transformed itself into a position where it wields considerable social influence.

Other institutions in society are less organized, less influential, and have significantly less tradition. The institution of recreation, for example, is not formally established in many social systems. Yet recreation is an important institution of society and plays a key role in the happiness of mankind. Recreation provides a human being with the relaxation and enjoyment necessary to ensure a well-rounded and satisfying life.

Institutions often overlap one another as they function to meet the needs of society. This is evident from an examination of two major institutions of social living, government and religion. The laws decreed by the state are based on the same values as the moral commitments promoted by the church. Both the institutions of government and religion tend to impose similar restrictions on human behavior. The members of society are expected to follow similar codes of conduct, whether secular or church-based.

Earlier we noted a society is nothing more than a collection of individual people. The institutions of society perform on an expanded scale what individuals perform at the singular level. There is no institution in society whose function isn't carried on by the individual person. Every man has his own government, religion, and means to earn a livelihood. Nevertheless, as noted previously, human beings accomplish more when working together in a social environment than they do by living alone.

Externally we can label an institution as government. We can describe how it's structured and how it functions in society. We can do a similar review of religion, employment, or any other institution of society. To do this on a personal level is to identify the main facets of human behavior. In everyday life a human being doesn't separate out his actions. A person does not categorize his behavior as to which institution it belongs. Neither does a person intentionally isolate his thought processes. He doesn't say, "I did this because of my religious outlook." Or, "I did that because of my political views." All the thoughts relevant to a person's behavior are housed together. Similarly, the "formal" institutions of society all belong together and function in unison to form a workable and lasting social structure.

Finally, mankind establishes institutions to promote order and unity as well as preserve the major advancements of social living. In the chapters ahead we will look at the institutions of mankind. We'll examine how these institutions are structured as well as highlight the functions they serve. Furthermore, we'll describe the direction the major institutions of society ought to be headed.

Modern man is specialized in both crafts and skills as it pertains to the employment sector of society. The structure of today's complex social-economic systems promotes specialization as a way of life. It's obvious that no human being can know everything there is to know in life. No human being can live long enough to know everything. Technology has grown so extensively that no person can learn everything there is to learn about a single physical science. No person can acquire all the knowledge there is to acquire in physics, chemistry, or biology. Likewise, no person can understand all there is understand about any of the social sciences, which means no one can learn all there is to learn about psychology, sociology, history, or law.

It's also obvious that no person can do everything that needs to be done. For instance, no single person can build an office building. Likewise, no individual working by himself can design and construct a supersonic airplane. No one person can grade a mountainside and lay down a highway. Further, no one person can journey to the moon. As we know, a trip to the moon requires the collaborative efforts of thousands of people working together within the aerospace industry. It takes a number of people specialized in their own fields to achieve major objectives in life. It takes dedicated individuals working side by side to make the major advancements of social living.

Specialization leads to the creation of a number of societal groups designed to promote opportunity and help man meet his needs. Man establishes industrial complexes which allow for the manufacture of a vast assortment of appliances and machinery to make life easier. He establishes transportation networks that allow for the rapid transfer of materials and products from one place to another. He further establishes communication networks which permit an efficient and convenient transfer of information across society. The ability to provide new materials, better products, and enhanced services allows mankind to develop a more accomplished mode of life. Furthermore, the installation of sound socio-economic systems enables man to expand and protect that mode of life.

Ever since the beginning of human history, man has continued to meet his biological and psychological needs. He does so essentially through one activity. That activity is work! No matter what generation one lives in, man works for what he wants. No matter what social structure one functions under, man works in order to survive. A caveman of 1,000,000 BC, a nomad of 100 BC, a serf of 1500 AD, a farmer of 1800 AD, and a factory employee of 2000 AD, all have one activity in common. Each person works to meet the biological and sociological requirements of his time.

Throughout history, the major needs of mankind do not change. What does change, however, is how man satisfies those needs. Hundreds of thousands of years ago man met his needs on an individual basis. For the most part, every man provided for himself and his family. Single-handedly, a person secured the necessary food, clothing, and shelter. In current times the means of maintaining one's well-being is much different than earlier times, for today a person meets nearly all his needs with the aid of his fellow man.

In modern times, just a small segment of the population constructs all of the houses people live in. Another segment produces all of the food people consume. A third segment of society manufactures all of the clothing apparel, and a fourth segment educates the children. A fifth segment maintains the legal system, and a sixth segment generates the energy that's needed to run society. And so it goes! Thousands of individual segments are in place across society to manufacture the products and provide the services required to keep the economy functioning.

At this point, we'll focus on the social world as a whole and not on its individual segments. There is an assortment of social systems in the world today and the world's societies tend to be stratified according to ethnic, religious, and political criteria. We note that the stratification is culturally based because biologically human beings are not separated. There is just one biological organism known as Homo sapiens. Likewise, racial distinctions identified as Caucasoid, Mongoloid, Negroid, Capoid, and Australoid are insignificant from a physiological standpoint. The only distinct physical difference with people is the sexual one, i.e., the difference of male and female. Not only are people physically the same but they are psychologically identical as well. Human beings are motivated by the same drives and needs, and they share the same mental facilities, both emotional and rational, in order to meet those needs. Interestingly, men and women are more alike from a psychological standpoint than they are in the biological sense.

There are a number of reasons why the societies of the world are diversified and none of them are because of biological factors. Rather they're based on environmental, cultural, and psychological factors. People are set apart in living habits due to the physical conditions of their environment. This has been aptly demonstrated by the major physical barriers of the world including mountains, oceans, and seas. There are some people who live on islands and others who live on mountain ranges. There are some people who live on the prairies and others who live in deserts. In past centuries, human beings didn't migrate very much because there were no convenient means of travel from one region to another. Another reason why people differ in social behavior is due to climatic conditions, which includes variations in the moisture content and temperature of the air. Indeed, the weather plays a significant role in the way people structure their lives. For instance, the Eskimos of cold arctic regions live in igloos made out of ice. The nomads of sandy desert areas live in tents made from sheepskin. And the Bushmen of the hot African jungles live in shelters made out of sticks and leaves. Another environmental reason why people differ culturally is due to the presence or absence of resources in their immediate region, which can affect the availability of food supplies. For example, the amount of fertile soil and level of minerals within the soil play a part. Also, the presence of sufficient sunshine and water are important. Further, the availability of fuel supplies, such as wood, coal, and oil, is significant in determining the way people live.

Because of various physical and environmental factors, people devise different ways to earn a living. For example, there are people who hunt and fish for a living. There are people who live on farms and grow food crops or raise livestock to support themselves. There are people who grow rice in patty fields that are laden with water. Further, there are people who live in cities and work in factories to manufacture a variety of consumable goods and products. Still other people work in the coal mines and gas fields to secure the fuel supplies needed to drive industry.

Additional reasons why people are diversified are based on cultural factors. Just as people come together to build a common social structure, once it's built, they also decide to keep their social structure separate from others. People wish to be different and consequently they stay apart by choice. People vary in their desires, tastes, attitudes, and interests. They establish and promote their own customs and beliefs. The result is a number of social structures with their own language, living habits, and methods of meeting socio-economic needs. Further, the people in these social structures determine their own set of values.

Some of the psychological factors responsible for the separation of people in the world include the following. Typically, they're built on prejudice, mistrust, fear, and lack of understanding. For whatever reason, some people don't like other people. It could be due to the way they look, speak, act, or think. Such psychologically-based reasons are the most unfair of all. Furthermore, they are the most detrimental to the success of commonality of purpose across the human race.

The diversification among people, as described above, has persisted for hundreds of thousands of years. At one time human beings were isolated in body and mind. The world's population was divided into separate entities as a result of environmental factors and people were separated because of hills, mountains, oceans, and seas. However, times changed and physical isolation no longer exists on a significant scale. Improvement in transportation has ended that kind of separation. There are highways which cross mountain ranges, ocean vessels that traverse the seas, and airplanes which take to the skies, thereby removing the barriers typically associated with land and water. There are non-physical factors which have kept people culturally isolated as well. However, modern advances in communication have helped bring an end to cultural isolation. Telegraph, telephone, radio, and television networks utilize satellite and computer systems on a worldwide basis. These communication mediums allow all regions of the world to interact in real time with one another.

Today, the only separation that remains among people is isolation based on psychological factors. There's an isolation of the mind due to social conditioning. It is driven by emotion and rooted in prejudice and mistrust. It's planned and taught. It is disruptive and must be overcome to allow the people of the world to achieve the common goals of humanity.

To ensure psychological-based isolation comes to an end, people must continue to learn about the cultures of others. Prejudices and biases which separate them have to be eliminated. The distrust and hatred due to cultural differences must cease and a universal acceptance of other people's way of life must come to pass. Hence, unhealthy sociologically-based feelings have to end if people everywhere are to unite and prosper.

The cultural unification of the world's population could occur over a long period of time and take hundreds, or even thousands, of years to complete. On the other hand, it can happen much quicker. Social unification could come about rather quickly if a common enemy of mankind were to appear on Earth. Assume for a moment that aliens from outer space came to Earth and began to enslave human beings. Suppose the aliens began to kill people and consume them as food. If this were to happen, the various nations of the world would unite quickly. The people would cooperate fully with one another and forget about their ethnic, religious, and political differences. Under a crisis situation like this, the people of the world would come together.

Eventually, the psychological isolation of man will disappear. It will happen when he shifts his priorities in life. Mankind is in a position to change focus, but to do so he must re-examine the values that drive human behavior. The world doesn't have to be invaded from outer space for people to realize it's important to change direction in life. The species of man already knows it has foes. In today's world mankind has a host of enemies to unite against. For instance ignorance, starvation, and poverty are our adversaries. Diabetes, tuberculosis, and typhoid fever are dangerous. The illnesses of heart disease, cancer, and AIDS are our natural enemies. Similarly air, water, and soil pollutants are detrimental to us. The effects of high energy radiation cause us harm. So too do the uses of toxins, poisons, and drugs. The crimes of assault, rape, and murder are our enemies. So too are deceit, lying, and intimidation. The conflicts of war destroy human limb and life. The effects resulting from physical injury and emotional harm are opponents to us. Likewise, depression and mental illness destroy our quality of life. All of these modern-day antagonists enslave and kill human beings just as predictable as a hostile alien would.

The people of the world must unite in a common cause to fight these enemies. The world's societies must cease their challenges to one another that are based on ethnic, religious, and political differences. Instead, the people of the world must unite and combat the present and common threats to all mankind.

Human beings are the same no matter where they live in the world. Although a number of social structures persist, the problems they all face remain the same. For instance, under a democracy or a monarchy the people must be protected from the criminal element. Inside a socialistic or a capitalistic-structured economy, the people require the means to provide food and shelter for themselves. Within a Hindu or Jewish culture, the people desire a sanctioned authority to conduct both matrimonial and funeral ceremonies. The various social structures of the world represent different preferences for meeting human needs. The individual societies represent different approaches to solving man's problems. There is much diversity to the people of the world and much diversity to their cultures. Nonetheless, human beings are essentially the same the world over and they share the same desire to live and prosper in the modern world.

A final word ought to be said about the diversity of the world's social structures as it relates to the common wishes of mankind. As the evolution of human culture proceeds, it's likely to end up as a homogeneous composition with one language, one nationality, one government, and one religion. This projection of homogeneity is based on the historical, developmental pattern of nearly all specie life. It's also based on the eventual merging of human values throughout the world as societal institutions which promote and support these values continue to mature. Although such a universal society of human beings may be desirable, it's not required. The diversity which exists among the people of the world isn't undesirable as long as the diversity doesn't lead to mistrust and hostility. There's no reason why individual societies cannot retain their own habits and customs and still work together to achieve man's purpose on Earth.

The ability to display Life, as a species is composed to do, make each and every species unique. The choice to display Life, as a species is supposed to do, make each and every species a valid representative of God. Interestingly, for each species of life, its many members are distinct and varied in their own right. As long as the members of a species don't fight or harm one another, they can live as they choose to live. Similarly, as long as members of the human race don't fight or harm one another, the world can retain its varied social structures and stay united in the pursuit of man's purpose in life. Thus, once united in peace, justice, equality, and respect, the people of the world can share the basic privilege of expressing themselves along the socio-cultural lines they cherish. As long as people follow the maxim of "live and let live", it's acceptable to maintain separate social structures throughout the world.

3

Family

THE MOST IMPORTANT INSTITUTION in society is the institution of family. It forms the nucleus of human social living. The family fosters a deep sense of commitment among biologically related people who live together in an emotionally secure environment. It's structured to meet the basic physiological and psychological needs of every person alive. Foremost, the family provides an opportunity, or home, around which love can and should be centered throughout a person's life.

Family life is extremely important to the happiness of the majority of people in the world and it provides the avenue through which the most rewarding human interactions can occur. The family provides for the meaningful expressions of warmth, affection, care, and concern. The strongest emotional bonds which can occur, the bonds of love, take place among the immediate members of a family. Indeed, the love between a husband and wife, a father and son, a mother and daughter, a sister and brother, represent the most meaningful emotional ties that can be formed.

The family represents the life-long union of two people committed together in love. It begins with the acceptance of the marriage vows by a man and woman. Their incentive to marry arises from the unparalleled love that's established between them. They develop common interests in life and their marriage is based on a unified set of values and beliefs. It is likewise founded on shared dreams and goals. The husband and wife commit to each other with a desire to stay married for life.

As we know, within any highly-developed animal species existing on Earth, God created the two sexes of male and female. Throughout Nature the male and female organisms come together, mate, and produce offspring. Thereby, a species continues and new organisms participate in the adventures of life. The human species is no exception, as men and women are biologically and psychologically designed to attract one another. A man and woman meet each other, date, become engaged, and marry. They join together and conceive a child. The woman carries the child and eventually gives birth. Biologically, the husband and wife are designed to create a family together. Psychologically, they're destined to raise their children in a family-based environment.

Typically, the family increases in size. This normally occurs with the birth of children, but it can take place by adoption as well. There is physical growth and emotional maturation within the family. Learning takes place as the family teaches its new members the skills they can use throughout their lives, such as writing, reading, math, carpentry, gardening, homemaking, and shopping. As the family grows it blossoms with new experiences. There is success and happiness as well as failure and sadness. And throughout it all, there's commitment and respect for one another. Further, there is one common thread which unites and sustains the family. That common, irreplaceable thread is love.

We're well aware the personality of a child is established early in life. All of one's inherited traits, physical and psychological, reside within the family. Likewise, many of the learned traits a person acquires are a result of family experiences. For example, the way a person walks is determined as a result of family training. So too is the way one talks. The way a person either laughs or cries is influenced by behaviors learned in a family relationship.

Without question, the dominant influence in a child's growth and development is that of the parents. The parents play a vital role in the way a child matures, both physically and psychologically. Responsible parents ensure the physical well-being of their children. Either one parent alone, or both together, work in the employment sector so the family can function and satisfy its economic needs. Both parents perform the maintenance tasks and daily services required to keep the household in order. The parents shop for groceries as well as purchase the shoes and clothing their children require. The parents cook the meals and wash the clothes. Further, they vacuum the carpets, clean the bathroom, and mow the lawn. Thereby, the mother and father maintain the home and provide stability to their children's lives.

As would be expected, a person's character is likewise molded by parental influence. Each parent provides leadership and teaches the importance of accountability. Each administers discipline and provides rules to live by. Likewise, both parents offer emotional support and moral guidance.

The parents are also the providers of joy and happiness. They pursue entertainment and recreational opportunities for their children to participate in.

Finally, the father and mother provide stability to the family by how they perform their parental duties. In a secure family structure, the parents are capable and committed. They are reasonable, fair, and compassionate. No doubt, the most important attribute parents possess is their ability to give unconditional love to their children.

Of all species of life, the human species dedicates the largest proportion of one's life to the parental care of offspring. Nearly a fourth of a person's life is spent as a dependent child under parental care. The first three or four years is spent with the parents meeting all of a child's needs, i.e., feeding, diaper changing, and teaching the child how to walk and talk. The next dozen or so years are spent with the child at home and in school, learning the skills needed to live and function in a social environment. During the developmental years, the child grows to physical and emotional maturity. Throughout this time the mother and father ensure the child's needs are met, in particular the biological needs of food, clothing, and shelter. The parents also ensure the child's emotional needs are satisfied, for they involve their son or daughter in recreational, sporting, and church-based activities. Even beyond the high school years the parents exert significant influence on a young person's life. For instance, a mother and father often provide their young adult with an automobile to drive or pay for the child's college expenses.

As illustrated, the immediate family structure remains intact for a considerable period of time. It's no wonder the family structure is so important to human development since the child is highly dependent upon his or her parents for so many years. During that period, there's a multitude of shared experiences between parent and child which reinforce the importance of the family structure.

No doubt, the overall manner as to how a person responds to life's situations is determined by the environment in which he develops. Needless to say, the key component of that environment is the family. The family represents the day-by-day, month-by-month, and year-by-year sharing of life's experiences. The sharing is time spent together performing numerous physical and social activities. The sharing also includes the exchange of emotional feelings, specifically the giving and receiving of love.

Family life consists of eating meals together, including early morning breakfasts and late afternoon dinners. It includes talking with one another about daily events associated with work, school, or playtime. Family life involves playing cards games such as canasta and hearts, as well as board games like Monopoly and Trivia Pursuit. Family life includes reading books, watching television, and listening to music together. It also entails helping with homework and saying prayers with each other at bedtime.

Family life involves going shopping, bowling, or to the movies together. It consists of going ice skating, sledding, or skiing with one another. It involves going to the park to play softball with one another, as well as swimming in the backyard pool. Also, family life takes place when playing tennis or golf together. Further, it consists of taking trips and vacations together.

Family life includes preparing for and hosting birthday parties, graduation parties, and neighborhood picnics. It involves having holiday dinners as well as family reunions. Family life also includes going to church together on Sunday.

Family life also consists of taking care of the house and outside property such as mowing the lawn, planting the flower and vegetable gardens, washing the car, etc. It involves assigning the household chores of washing dishes, doing the laundry, taking out garbage, and so forth.

Family life consists of being supportive of family members. It encompasses the emotions which arise whenever family members engage in new endeavors. For example, family life is evident in the expressions of joy a parent displays as a baby takes his or her first steps. It's demonstrated in the ensuing applause when a child is able to ride his or her bike without help. It's seen in the shedding of tears as a first grader climbs aboard the school bus on the opening day of school. It's obvious in the excitement expressed for a son when he hits his first home run in a little league baseball game. It is apparent in the pride shown in a daughter when she flawlessly completes her first piano recital. Family life is further evident in the sense of accomplishment in a handshake, or hug, for a high school senior on graduation day. It's apparent by the tear in one's eye when saying goodbye to a young man or woman about to leave home and begin college. It's demonstrated in the feeling of happiness on learning one's son has been offered a new job in the career field he really enjoys. It's shown in the pride of walking your daughter down the aisle on her wedding day. It is obvious from the thrill of holding a baby grandson or granddaughter in your arms for the first time.

Similarly, family life involves being grateful and relieved as your mother recovers from a surgery or serious illness. It's visible in the anticipation and excitement when your father drives home in a newly purchased automobile. It also entails the feeling of sadness and loss when your grandmother or grandfather passes away.

The house one lives in plays a role in family unity and forms a key part of the family's identity. This includes not only the building itself but the adjoining property. It can involve the property like one's front yard. It can involve land such as the farmland where members of the family help plow fields, plant seeds, and harvest crops. Just as a person's heart is bound to family members, so one's heart is tied to the home he grew up in. It may be an apartment building in the city with a fire escape and roof where one spends hot summer evenings. It may be a house in the suburbs with a front and back yard where one plays badminton, croquet, and kickball while growing up. It may consist of a farmhouse and barn in the country with rolling fields and wooded hillsides where one runs and explores as a child.

For sure, the house and property comprise the home. It belongs to the family and brings cohesiveness to the family structure. Along with the family itself, the house serves as an abode of security throughout a person's life.

The family unit is the center of social living. Although the family is the most important institution in society it doesn't exist independent of other institutions. As with the institution of religion, the family provides moral direction in life. The family provides the child with a basis for spiritual guidance and moral behavior. Like the institution of government, the family instills discipline. The family teaches a child the importance of following the rules and being responsible for your actions. And similar to the institution of education, the family prepares a young person for successful entry into the social world. The family teaches a young person the fundamental skills of reading, writing, spelling, and arithmetic.

The family unit is vital to sustaining a strong social environment. As we said, the core family unit consists of a man and woman bonded in marriage. The husband and wife are united in the pursuit of values covering all aspects of social living which range from education and employment, to politics and religion, to entertainment and recreation. Following marriage, the family unit grows in size to include the immediate members, i.e., the children, either conceived by the parents and borne by the mother, or adopted into the family. The family unit extends to the parents and grandparents of the husband and wife as well. Over time, the family increases with the addition of spouses who end up marrying the adult children. Thereafter, the family grows with the arrival of grandchildren. Eventually the spouses of the grandchildren are added, and with the arrival of great grandchildren, the family retains its place as the singly most important unit of society.

4

Religion

OTHER THAN THE INSTITUTION of family, the two social institutions that have the greatest influence upon the lives of people are the institutions of religion and government. Traditionally, religion and government play major roles in the development of human culture on Earth. In general, religion is concerned with placing sanctions on moral behavior. Religion defines morality and authorizes correct human behavior. It further determines that proper behavior is conduct which meets the approval of the ultimate provider of life, God. Religion is the conduit that ties human behavior to morality, the importance of life, and the creator of the universe. It serves as the pathway for interaction between an individual and his or her God. Government, on the other hand, is concerned with human behavior as it pertains to temporal interactions. Government defines human behavior which is proper and fair to individuals throughout society. It tries to establish a standardized code of justice and equity which is suitable to a social environment. Government is the conduit for proper behavior between man and his fellow man. As with other major institutions, the workings of religion and government are interconnected and interwoven into every facet of social living.

We noted earlier that a basic feature of the non-biological nature of man lies in the emphasis placed upon value. Life appears valuable and of special worth. It's important to understand Life's special worth as people seek to comprehend the origins of animate life and basis for their own existence. The quest to unlock the fundamental reasons for life on Earth plays a key role in the formation of religious doctrine.

Hence, understanding the underlying basis for animate life is important to mankind. Also important is an appreciation of the domain that life occupies. The universe houses billions upon billions of stars and planets.

The sun, a single star, maintains its own family of planets. A single planet, Earth, maintains itself as an abode for specie life. All of these realms are of major interest to man. Centuries ago, mankind became aware of the vastness of the universe as well as the unique events that occur within it. Man's study of this magnificent universe fuels his desire to understand the basis and meaning to all reality.

Man is aware of the majesty of the universe and he looks for the underlying authority behind it. He wonders who has the insight to design this cosmos as well as the power and capability to build it. Whatever the force, or whoever the source, mankind is in awe. As human culture progressed, it didn't take long for mankind to develop a reverence for the creator. The maker of the universe has to be much more intelligent, more capable, and more powerful than mortal man.

Man's desire to understand the basis of life leads to investigations on the workings of Nature. The investigations, in turn, lead to the formation of philosophical views about the world. The philosophical views originate from several sources. Some philosophical views arise out of ignorance. Other views emanate from a fear of the unknown. Likewise, some are derived from mysticism. Some are derived from a spiritual association with undefined phenomena in Nature. Further, there are intellectually founded world views derived from experience and based on a rational study of forces and events in Nature. Finally, there are world views believed to be given to man by God, either directly or through an agent, that is, a religious leader. Regardless of the source, however, worldviews reflect many similar features, one of which is the fact they contain a strong emotive element. Worldviews are founded on faith and over time many of them evolve into religious dogmas.

All major worldviews determine there's an underlying force to the universe. All views typically identify that force as a creator or a supreme being. Additionally, the worldviews attach some type of religious veneration to it. The major worldviews further recognize there's uniqueness to life. Consequently, they seek to attach meaning and value to the human experience on Earth. Appropriately, they make the necessary linkages between human life and its creator.

A philosophical view that developed centuries ago in India was Brahmanism. The followers of Brahmanism believed their god, Brahman, was the essence of the universe. Brahman was the ultimate substance from which reality was created. According to Brahmanism, everything in the universe is a manifestation of a single entity. That included all creatures of life. It included all nonliving objects as well.

On a macro level, Brahman encompassed all of creation. Brahman was infinite in extent for there was no sector of the universe that lacked its presence. Brahman was eternal in duration as there was no period of time when it didn't exist. Brahman was also self-sustaining. It maintained itself and everything under its influence. Stars and planets as well as events in Nature proceeded according to principles laid down by Brahman. On a personal level, the influence of Brahmanism encompassed every aspect of man's nature. For example, the skin and bone of man were extensions of Brahman. So too were the mental aspects of the human mind. The entire human organism was one with the ultimate Brahman.

Through philosophies such as Brahmanism mankind devises major theories about the universe and its creator. He states suppositions about the forces at work in Nature and through such philosophies expresses beliefs about the importance of life on Earth.

Mankind molds philosophical beliefs into dogmas of sacredness and holiness. And with time, world religions are born. The teachings of Brahmanism, for example, eventually led to the formation of the Hindu religion. Most major religions, like Hinduism, become the avenue through which mankind establishes a moral order to the universe. Similarly, most religions become the means to instruct people on how to add value to their life.

As human culture evolves, religious development follows a predictable trend. The social structures from the most primitive to the most complex adopt beliefs in some type of ecclesiastical doctrine. Within society, an established religion increases in size and domain. Not only does membership rise but its doctrine grows as well. In general, man's religious thesis expands into areas beyond acknowledgement of the omnipotent characteristics of God. It likewise expands into areas beyond the singular connection identified between Nature and man. What typically happens is that a religious thesis takes on the role of monitoring relationships occurring among people as they participate in everyday situations. Thusly, social interaction becomes tied to religious protocol.

Over time the religions become institutionalized and churches, temples, and mosques are formed. Within the church, etc., a set of formalized procedures is established. Holy days are decided and rites and rituals are determined. That is, religions define the conditions for marriage and the church performs the wedding ceremonies. The church conducts rites of dedication which includes baptisms and bar mitzvahs. Likewise, the church takes on the responsibility for memorial and funeral services. The place and time for worship service are established. The Sunday schools and adult religious classes are put in place. Similarly, the amount of monetary support which church members ought to provide is determined.

As religions expand their sphere of influence, they become involved in a number of social matters. Most religions attempt to, or wish to, regulate everyday human behavior. For example, they may determine the types of food people can consume, which is typically specified on a weekly, monthly, or holiday basis. Religions may also determine the type of footwear, clothing, and headdress people ought to wear. Further, they attempt to set limits on the nature and extent of sexual activity as it pertains to marriage and one's marital status. That is, religions define adultery and set the conditions for divorce. Additionally, religions determine the time and manner by which people ought to pay homage to the church's hierarchy. Further, the world's religions publish treatises on a variety of human behavioral subjects including love, compassion, and humility. The religions issue decrees on political matters as well. From generation to generation, the world religions play a major role in the lives of people. For the most part, religions provide spiritual guidance and give millions upon millions of people the incentive to live a decent and moral life on Earth.

As with every other major institution in society, the institution of religion is highly diversified. There are a number of religions each with its own view in regard to the creative force behind the universe. Likewise, there are a number of religions each with its own view as to the state of Nature and man's place in it. Similarly, there are a number of religions each with its own complement of sacraments, rituals, and rites. At this point, we'll look at several religions of the world, past and present, to see if we can find some common grounds to them. Specifically, we'll look to see if there're certain areas of belief which could be combined to form a universal religion for mankind. Important areas of concern for most religions are outlined below.

One dominant feature the religions of the world share is the belief in a god, or gods, as the ultimate creative force behind the world and its inhabitants. Religions always advocate a belief in a divine entity controlling the universe. The religions attempt to determine what this entity, i.e., Supreme Being, is composed of.

A major feature of the religion of Sikhism is the belief in a single omnipotent god. According to the doctrine of Sikhism, there is one god who presides over the universe and everything in it. This god is eternal. He is the creator of all beings, and according to Sikhism, places mankind at the topmost level in the hierarchy of animate life on Earth.

The religion of Judaism holds that the universe is created by one god. According to the Jewish religion this god is the only god in existence. The Jewish god is all-powerful and all-knowing. People who adhere to the Jewish faith believe that God holds human beings responsible for their actions. In other words, God serves as the judge of human behavior, and to achieve salvation in the afterlife the members of the Jewish faith must purify their soul. According to Judaism, mankind should strive to attain moral perfection on Earth.

The god of Christianity is similar to the god of Sikhism and Judaism. The Christian god is all-creative, all-knowing, and all-powerful. Furthermore, God is eternal. A key feature of Christianity is the conviction that God has already appeared on Earth. He manifested himself as a human being over two thousand years ago. Christ, the son of God, walked among the common people and through his presence demonstrated the value of human existence. A basic principle of Christian doctrine is the belief that God is infinitely good and will offer salvation to anyone who truly believes in him.

Most religions express a belief in the existence of a god who runs the universe. Religions express the belief that a divine being also controls the actions of man. All religions require the believers of their faith to show reverence to God and the manner by which one shows reverence is very important. For example, a member of the Islamic faith must pray to Allah five times a day.

Hence, we recognize that every major religion stresses the need for man to show proper respect to his creator. People have strong feelings about the relationships between themselves and God, and the religions of the world offer an avenue for the expression of such feelings. Indeed, many of man's feelings on the creation of the universe, as well as its creator, are encompassed in spiritual values. The term which describes the ultimate religious value is the word holy. Every religion holds its god to be holy. Every religion holds certain rituals that it performs as being sacred. By way of human actions which acknowledge the concepts of holiness and sacredness, mankind pays respect to his god. Mankind worships him, venerates him, and communicates with him through prayer.

The range of objects for veneration shown by the people has changed throughout history. For example, many of the earlier religions were polytheistic in nature. Those religions assigned spiritual powers to forces in Nature across a broad spectrum. The believers of the early religions worshipped a multitude of beings and objects. They worshiped animals, trees, mountains, lakes, and waterfalls. They even worshiped geologically-crafted structures of rock and stone. Similarly, some of the world's earlier religions held the belief in mana, a belief in the presence of various spirits in non-living things. Still other religions gave credence to animism stating that everything in the world, animate beings and inanimate objects, possessed a soul. A cultural group that held veneration for an assortment of objects was the Celts of Medieval England. The Celts believed all objects were sacred and they worshipped nearly everything found in their surroundings.

More recent religions tend to focus their veneration on a single entity. This single entity is always identified as the ultimate creative force behind the universe. However defined, it is God. Thus, the various religions of the world are concerned with describing a creator of the universe and then they go on to honor the creator through worship and prayer.

In addition to a desire to explain the ultimate creative force behind the universe, religions are concerned with the way the universe operates. Many religions study the workings of Nature and attempt to assign a cause-effect relationship between the laws of Nature and the human experience on Earth. Such religions seek a homeostatic balance between Nature and the world of man.

The Far Eastern religion of Taoism expresses a philosophy based upon the orderliness of the universe. According to Taoism, the entire universe of stars and planets operates under definite laws. Basically, they are the laws of Nature. From a scientific perspective they would include the law of inertia, the law of universal gravitation, the laws of conservation of matter and energy, etc. The believers of Taoism say that if the laws of Nature are followed then the universe functions as it should. Events take place in a prescribed and sound fashion. Thereby, everything in the universe is in harmony.

According to its believers, every species of life should adhere to the principles of Taoism. This includes the human species as well. The underlying premise of this philosophy is that mankind will find harmony in life through adherence to the methodical workings of Nature. As it turns out, Taoism is just one example of a religious philosophy that ties harmony in Nature to the successful spiritual fulfillment of a person's life on Earth.

Another major feature of the religions of the world deals with the issue of human worth. This aspect is centered on a perceived level of quality placed upon man's soul. With a negative focus, some religions express the belief that man is inherently sinful. They preach man should continually seek improvement in the quest for moral perfection in life. For those religions, every person should commit himself to the expulsion of evilness from both body and mind. Conversely, on the positive slant there are world religions which hold the belief that man's soul is essentially good. These religions place emphasis upon the value of the human experience on Earth. Such religions derive an inner glory through the recognition and promotion of human worth.

A major religion of the Orient, Confucianism, places a strong emphasis upon the basic goodness of mankind. According to the teachings of Confucianism, everyone is assigned a certain station in life. Each person needs to understand his role and behave in a manner that brings fulfillment to that role. Human relationships are extremely important and everyone must in an honest and forthright manner appreciate the situation of others. Young people should pay respect to the elderly. A child should honor and obey his parents. An employee should likewise hold his employer in high regard. Across society people must exhibit respect, concern, and support for one another. The doctrine of Confucianism predicts such behavior will allow people to experience a greater understanding and appreciation of life.

Another religion strongly tied to the concept of human worth is Christianity. According to Christian belief, the true meaning of life can be found within one's heart. The basis for everything good in life is love. Love for one's fellow man is a desirable goal and the believer of Christianity takes satisfaction in being able to forgive one's transgressors. The Christian heart is believed to be unlimited in its capacity to display this humanitarian-type love.

Indeed, a belief in the basic goodness of mankind is held by many religions. However, no major religion states that a human being is a perfect creature. People do err and make mistakes. People need guidance and direction in their daily lives. In all cases, that direction is tied to proper moral behavior. Moral behavior is a key principle to the world's religious doctrine, and appropriately, many religions offer rules of conduct identifying ethical human behavior.

The Islamic religion lists a number of duties its followers should perform in order to attain moral correctness. For example, the members of the

Islamic faith are expected to continually declare their belief in the existence of an omnipotent, omniscient, and singular God. This God is Allah. They should accept the writings in the Koran as the true words of God, and they should ascribe to the understanding that Mohammed is the single prophet of Allah. In regard to moral duty, the members of the Islamic faith are expected to provide aid to the poor and needy members of society. Additionally, Islamic followers are instructed to pray five times a day. Likewise, they should fast throughout the sacred period of Ramadan, and if possible, pilgrimage to Mecca at least once in their lifetime.

Rules of conduct are instructions on what people should or should not do in order to live a moral life. The instructions can be a list of positive behaviors which if followed would ensure a moral life. Conversely, the instructions can delineate undesired behaviors which if pursued would prevent the attainment of a moral life. For many religions, the rules of conduct often focus on behavior that is unacceptable and negative in nature.

Examples of religions that provide rules on what people shouldn't do are Buddhism and Jainism. The Buddhists are taught that is wrong to lie and steal. It is wrong to commit adultery. It is wrong to kill. Further, Buddhists are taught that it is wrong to participate in foolish-type activities such as singing and dancing. It is also wrong to consume alcoholic beverages. It is wrong to dress and act in a sexually-enticing manner. The rules of Jainism are similarly prohibitive. The followers of Jainism are taught not to lie or steal. Similarly, the Jainists are instructed not to commit adultery. They are not supposed to kill. Like the Buddhists, the Jainists are not to indulge in extravagant or obnoxious behavior. They are not to pursue excessive nor self-gratifying activities, and they're taught not to amass material wealth.

The Judeo-Christian religions also provide a negatively based "code of conduct". The Judeo-Christian code is the Ten Commandments. The commandments provide a set of rules to follow if the person wants to lead a moral life. For the most part, the commandments represent a list of "thou shall not" rather than a list of "thou shall" directives. Again, the majority of entries on the list identify specific activities and behaviors that are unacceptable. Although it's okay to have a list of "thou shall not" directives, any set of moral guidelines should include a list of "thou shall" directives as well.

Another major feature of a number of religions in the world is the belief in a life-after-death. These religions state that a person who lives a moral life can transmigrate to an afterlife. In the afterlife the individual will be reunited with other moral people, and once there, he or she will share in eternal bliss with God.

Redemption and salvation are the religious avenues to an afterlife, and in order to gain access, exemplary moral behavior is required on Earth. As stated above, the so-called "rules of conduct" offer instruction on proper moral behavior. Presumably, by adhering to these religious codes, people earn the opportunity to enter into the life hereafter. For example, the religion of Jainism requires intense self-discipline from its followers. According to Jainism one must remain innocent of immoral conduct. One must not harm the life of any living creature. If a believer of Jainism lives as instructed, he or she will have an opportunity for salvation. Similarly, if a member of the Hindu faith wants to attain salvation, he must meet specific religious requirements. For one, he must acquire knowledge. For another, he must meditate. Further, as an overall directive a Hindu follower must continually practice rituals verifying his devotion to God.

As seen from our discussion, there are several key features common to the major religions of the world. Each religion defines the spiritual realm in its own way. Each religion offers its own perspective in regard to the human experience on Earth. Many religions were established throughout the course of history, and in general, most of them have been beneficial to their followers. Most religions spiritually guide their believers to successfully navigate the straits of human temptation on Earth. Given the complexity of human culture, it's not undesirable to have a variety of religions available to mankind. As we know, the societies of the world are diversified. The customs and habits of people vary. Religious beliefs, along with other areas of human endeavor, change from social structure to social structure and from one era to another.

Although there are a number of religions with varying beliefs and traditions, they're alike in the service they provide and role they play in the history of mankind. Each major religion attempts to assist mankind in the quest for spiritual enlightenment. Each attempts to provide human beings with a sense of moral security. And each religion attempts to seal the bond between humanity and its creator. Thus, it's necessary that every religion satisfies the function for which it's intended, and that it meets the spiritual needs of the people and social structure it serves.

It's acceptable for each religion to independently pledge allegiance to a specific and predefined deity. Nonetheless, all religions ought to ascribe to a universal force of creativity. It's appropriate that each religion has a unique approach to Nature, Life, and the role of mankind. Nonetheless, all religions should be united in basic concepts about Life's interrelations and the value of human existence on Earth. It's alright for each religion to subscribe to a given set of dogma. Nonetheless, all religions ought to share in certain fundamental spiritual beliefs. Further, it's suitable that each religion specializes in its own rituals and ceremonies. However, all religions should overlap in areas which promote acceptable social conduct.

Collectively, the major religions of the world contain the main body of doctrine pertinent to a universal religion. As we examine the various religions, we can identify the basic elements which would comprise the foundation of a universal religion. We can sort out, rearrange, and combine them. We can also make some elements less or more specific. From this endeavor, we can speculate on what a universal religion should be like. Such a religion would serve any individual at any time in human history.

The universal religion is a religion for all mankind. The universal religion isn't specialized to conform to certain theologies; rather it accommodates the general spiritual beliefs of people everywhere. It knows no external structure such as the church. However, it may have such a structure. It knows no rituals and no ceremony. Nonetheless, it may have such ceremony. For the most part, the basis of a universal religion is found internally as it resides within the heart of mankind.

Let's review some key elements of the institutionalized religions we've discussed, and from the review, we'll select elements which can be used to characterize a universal religion. First, let's look at the belief in the existence of God. Most religions express a belief in God and so should a universal religion.

There is a God. Of this there can be no doubt. There often arise questions in regards to God's nature, specifically questions about his qualities and capabilities. For many religions, God is basically an eternal being with infinite power, knowledge, and goodness. This God created and operates the universe. And as long as the world's religions accept the principle of God as the underlying force of creation, they are doing God justice.

Many religions postulate that events in Nature are ordained by a supreme being. Regarding the control of events by a divine power, consider the following. The events of Nature are described through the laws of science. Astronomy, chemistry, physics, mathematics, and related sciences delineate how the universe functions. The reason why scientific laws are written the way they are is because these laws describe the "system" as it operates. They describe how the system actually functions. The system in this case is the Animate Form of Life. The creator behind the Animate Form of Life, in turn, is GOD. Thus, God controls events in Nature to the extend he determines and changes, if necessary, the rules by which it operates.

Another major premise of religious doctrine centers on the belief that God intervenes in human affairs. Many religions share the belief that God controls human destiny. Further, many religions contend that God is directly involved in everyday social interactions. Presumably, God rewards people when they are good to one another and he punishes them when they are not. These religions theorize that someday God will come to Earth to judge all mankind. As the ultimate reward, God will offer eternal salvation to those who lead a moral life and believe in him.

For the most part, the religions say God has not yet come to Earth for the final judgment. Nevertheless, there are some religions that believe God has already visited Earth. For example, the Christian religion states that Christ, as the son of God, appeared on Earth over two thousand years ago to deliver people from sin and provide them with an avenue to heaven. Similar to Christianity, there are other religions that believe God does manifest himself in human form. Consider the other great religious leaders like Buddha, Moses, Muhammad, and Confucius. All of these leaders are believed to have divine qualities. All of them are thought to have divine contact. The people who adhere to their respective religions believe that God does intervene directly in human affairs through such great religious leaders. Indeed this may be true!

What if religious leaders, such as Christ, are divine and have already appeared on Earth? Does it matter if they were here one or more times before? Conversely, what if the religious leaders like those mentioned above are only men? What if these leaders have no divine or supernatural qualities? In that case, is it likely God doesn't appear nor intervene directly on Earth? But does it matter either way? Does it matter whether or not God participates directly in human affairs? Does it matter whether or not God intervenes in man's daily activities on Earth? Not really!

If God has or has not intervened in human affairs to date, should the world's societies worry about it? To ask a more pertinent question, should the waiting for divine intervention preclude human action on its own? The answer is, "Not in the least!" In regard to taking initiative action, what should people do? Should people wait for God's intervention, or should they attempt to change the moral fabric of society on their own? We do have a choice! Whenever people want to make improvements on Earth they can sit and wait and pray. Or, they can do more. People can attempt to bring about the changes they would expect God to make!

The role of God should be projected into the deeds of mankind. It is really the responsibility of people on Earth to achieve God's goals and make improvements in life. A man must try to change the world of man. Then, if God does come to Earth the people will already have given him a hand. Thereby, people will give God a head start with his tasks.

In actuality, when we attempt to improve the quality of moral and spiritual life on Earth, it's inherently being directed by God anyhow, because we are God's representatives on Earth doing what he has created us to do. We are doing what we are biologically composed to do and psychology supposed to do; and we're doing it because of the presence in our being of a universal soul, i.e., the soul of God. So our actions involve God's bidding whether he has been here before or not.

Human beings are directed by their innate nature to enhance the quality of life. Human beings are also directed through the various religions of the world to improve social living. The people must continue to expand upon their religious dogmas of Taoism, Judaism, Buddhism, Hinduism, Islamism, Christianity, etc. We must continue to apply religious teachings to a changing social world.

Current institutionalized religions are serving the spiritual needs of man, and the emphasis they place on holiness and moral worth doesn't change over time. For sure, reverence to a deity is the keystone to the major religions of the world. Likewise, the practice of human morality lies at the heart of the religious experience on Earth.

All institutionalized religions should permit membership to anyone who wishes to join them. A religion cannot exclude a human being from its spiritual envelope because of age, sex, or skin color. Likewise, a religion cannot exclude a person due to social background, ethnical heritage, or political allegiance. No institutionalized religion should offer salvation to a group of selected individuals. Salvation cannot be made available only to individuals who repent of their sins. Instead, salvation must be available to all. The baby who dies at birth should be entitled the same redemption as the Muslim who prays five times a day. Similarly, the heathen aborigine of Australia who follows no rituals must receive the same salvation as the Orthodox Jew, who conscientiously performs weekly sacraments. The insane person in a mental hospital, who never experiences religious training, must go to the same heaven as the Christian who reverently attends church every Sunday. Institutionalized religions must be available to provide spiritual support to any human being who's in need. Just as every institutionalized religion ought to be open to accept anyone, a universal religion must be totally inclusive and provide an avenue of spiritual fulfillment to everyone who would believe.

We should look at how a universal religion might be structured relative to the framework of the current religions of the world. Regarding rules to live by, a universal religion should have goals that are attainable. A shortcoming of many institutionalized religions is they have goals that are completely out of reach of a human being. We've already discussed one religion that has some rather specific, yet unattainable goals. That religion is the Christian religion. Through his teachings Christ gave direction on how people ought to live. Through his life Christ gave an example of what is proper moral conduct. However, many of his followers have put certain behavioral demands above normal human capability. For example, it's recognized that sin can occur through action alone, and through thought and action together. Even more so, it can singly occur in one's thought where evil thoughts are equated to performing evil deeds. In the Bible it states " . . . whosoever looketh on a woman to lust after her hath committed adultery with her already in his heart."[1] The goal then is to eliminate bad or evil thoughts from one's mind (or heart) since the inference is that evil thoughts are, in and of themselves, evil. Although human beings have the ability to refrain from committing wrongful acts, it's virtually impossible for twenty-first century man not to think of committing sin.

We pursue both attainable and unattainable goals, and it's commendable that we do so. However, some of the goals laid down by Scripture cannot presently be attained by mankind. These goals may never be attained by human beings. To live a life that is one hundred percent moral in body, mind, and spirit is worthy of pursuit, but not necessarily attainable. If the attainment of moral perfection in both thought and deed requires evolution, then the species of mankind hasn't evolved to that point yet. In setting its moral sights on a high plane, a universal religion must fittingly establish goals that are achievable.

Further, a universal religion must be designed to champion a positive approach to life. The pursuit of self-actualization must be an enjoyable pursuit. At times, the various institutionalized religions espouse a negative approach towards human behavior. Many of the rules people live by are rules that prohibit action and too often a religion tells people what they

---

1. *The Holy Bible, King James Version*. N. T. Matt, 5:28.

cannot do. Instead, a religion should tell people what they can do. The institutionalized religions ought to instruct people on activities that are worthy of pursuit.

A similarly negative approach involves the emphasis certain institutionalized religions place upon the value of life on Earth. In many cases the importance of our temporal existence is subordinated significantly. Too often, penance and deliverance are the behavior-driving objectives of a religion. Too often, the focus is to help prepare a person for a life-hereafter rather than provide the person with the guidance to achieve moral success on Earth. Too often, a person isn't supported enough to feel emotionally secure in this life. Too often, a person is not encouraged to enjoy the world-experience in its current state.

Accompanying a prevailing negative emphasis on temporal existence is the assumption that mankind is inherently evil. Many religions assume this theological-philosophical position. It is true that the human character isn't perfect and people do makes mistakes. However, too many times religious leaders tell us how sinful we are. Unfortunately, spread across a significant body of religious doctrine is the premise that man's innate character is morally flawed. This isn't true, for mankind is not inherently sinful. Instead, he makes mistakes. Man's innate nature is basically good and his life on Earth is meaningful. His temporal living is truly a positive experience.

Basically, mankind is good and his life on Earth is important. The thrust of religion should be forward looking in its approach to morality. What mankind needs is a list of positive endeavors to undertake, and a universal religion can provide that list. A universal religion can define the moral convictions suited to man's success on Earth. Additionally, a universal religion can mold human behavior to pursue the moral convictions that are achievable.

We know that a human being is a creature of action. We've indicated man's energies must be directed to positive ends. It can justly be asked, what are the positive ends that mankind ought to pursue? Some positive behaviors which mankind should embrace to achieve moral perfection on Earth are given below.

- A person should maintain a positive outlook on life. He should be outgoing. He should promote accomplishment and success.
- A person should work hard. He should put forth the required effort to accomplish goals. He should be conscientious and dedicated. He should perform his duties with conviction.

- A person should be trustworthy. He should be honest and always tell the truth.
- A person should be kind and polite. He should show respect to other people. He should honor his parents and grandparents.
- A person ought to exude love. He should love his family and friends. He should openly demonstrate to the people he loves that he loves them.
- A person should be compassionate. He should demonstrate care and concern for his fellow man.
- A person should aid others in the pursuit of an education. He should volunteer in nursery schools, elementary and secondary schools, colleges and universities, and other institutes of learning to help people attain a well-rounded education.
- A person should strive to improve the health care of others. He should donate his time and resources to help people in hospitals, nursing homes, and other medical facilities. He should offer physical and emotional support to those who are ill.
- A person should serve his community. He should do volunteer work in charitable organizations to provide food, clothing, and shelter for the needy. Through involvement in a social service organization, he should ensure the necessities of life are available to everyone.
- A person ought to take care of other creatures of life. He should take care of his pets. He should promote the survival of other species of animals in the world.
- A person should help preserve the environment. He should landscape and beautify the land.
- Not lastly, a person ought to enjoy life. He should pursue happiness and engage in fun activities with his family and friends. He should be satisfied with his life.

These ends are within the reach of all people living on Earth. When mankind is able to achieve these and similar goals, he will have found human perfection. These represent the basic objectives of a universal religion for mankind. Achieving these objectives will secure the completeness of man as envisioned by God.

The point of the above discussion is to show that religions of the world should emphasize positive steps to be taken rather than focus on negative prohibitions when it comes to good moral behavior. This is important to the human race. However, we mustn't lose sight of the fact that prohibitions espoused via ecclesiastical doctrine are significant. Indeed, the behaviors a person should adhere to include the lists of "thou shall not", such as not killing another, not lying, not stealing, not raping, and not causing harm to someone in physical or emotional ways. These are just as important as the pursuit of the positive actions we're promoting. Nonetheless, to avoid negative admonishments, and to entertain positive directives in life, make for happier individuals.

Everyone seeks a spiritual focus in life. No person can identify himself as a disbeliever relative to the need for spiritual leadership and moral guidance. Religion in one design or another is necessary for the species of mankind. Religion declares the meaningfulness of life. It provides the emotional security that's required for a human being created in the animate world. Mankind can use religion to recognize the beauty of this life. He can utilize religion to relate to the majesty of the universe and its creation. Finally, and most importantly, mankind can utilize religion to acknowledge and revere the existence of God.

The future direction of the culture of man lies within the will of man. We know that mankind has the opportunity to establish a universal religion. We also know he has the will. Everyone needs peace of mind, and one of the main goals of a universal religion is to provide mankind with emotional security. Everyone also needs the confidence to pursue two directives in life. One directive is aimed at experiencing a happy and satisfied life. The other is helping to achieve one's purpose in life.

It must be emphasized that a universal religion, as any of the universal institutions we discuss, should only come about because of people's desire to develop it voluntarily. It should never come about due to intimidation, coercion, or forced acceptance by either physical conquest or mental indoctrination.

A universal religion can provide mankind with spiritual guidance. Likewise, it can supply man with the vitality of character that's needed to work and function in the world. A universal religion can provide man with encouragement to perform good deeds. Also, it can help man restructure society to improve his overall quality of life.

No human being then can forego the benefits of a universal religion. With the aid of a universal religion, mankind can better understand and focus on his role in life. Mankind can use religion to realize the value of temporal existence. With that realization, he can help improve the welfare of all people. Mankind can likewise utilize religion to acknowledge the equality of animate life. With that recognition he can help promote and protect the well-being of all living creatures.

5

Government

GOVERNMENT HAS A MAJOR influence upon the lives of people. Its role is to maintain an environment suitable for the conduct of "proper" human behavior, and consequently, institutional governments are established to provide such an environment. Institutional governments draw up and enact rules for acceptable social behavior. Government further has the responsibility to protect human rights and institutional governments are designed to do that. For instance, they afford the privilege to acquire and own property. They also ensure citizens have the right to vote on important issues of the day. Government further provides an atmosphere for economic and social opportunity. Institutional governments appropriately promote this by allowing a person to seek a job of one's choosing, as well as purchase a home in a neighborhood where he or she wishes to live. Government is likewise designed to maintain social order, and in support of this, institutional governments provide for an individual's well-being through the installation of a police force and a system of civil and criminal courts. Thus, the role of all institutional governments is to guarantee a controlled social environment wherein people can interact satisfactorily with one another.

In the previous chapter, we discussed the institution of religion and determined that one universal religion could be held by all mankind. This we can define. We can draw from the several major institutional religions of the world to formulate a theological doctrine that would form the basis of a universal religion. Similarly, there can be one universal government in the world. This too we can define. We can select specific legislative, executive, and judicial components from various world governments to lay the foundation for a universal government. Such a government, which is responsive to the needs of all mankind, can be established on Earth.

The institutions of government and religion are alike in that both are concerned with "correct" behavior. Religion's emphasis focuses on behavior that's founded on moral principles. Its approach is spiritually based and tied to a belief in and obedience to a supreme being. Government's emphasis pertains to behavior that's founded on the precepts of justice. Government's approach is secular and tries to establish a common basis for equality and fairness among the citizens. Where the goal of the institution of religion is a moral world, the role of the institution of government is a just world.

As might be expected religion and government overlap each other in several key areas. At their foundation, both have a strong sense of commitment to the importance of "good" behavior. The value "thou shall not kill" applies to religion. To murder a human being is a sin specifically delineated in all religious doctrine. This value applies to the institution of government as well. To murder another person is a crime against society, and as such, it's punishable through the nation's system of law enforcement agencies, courts, and penal institutions.

Religion and government are further similar in that each offers a "code of conduct" to follow. Religion's code centers on moral behavior. It's tied directly or indirectly to a power outside this world, namely God. Government's code, on the other hand, is concerned with more temporal issues. Government's code deals with social interaction and addresses such topics as debts, property rights, and the equitable transfer of goods and services.

All the institutional governments of the world begin with natural government. Likewise, the universal government of mankind has natural government at its foundation. At this point, it's worthwhile to discuss some basic features of natural government. In doing this, we should begin by asking what is natural government and where does it occur?

Natural government is the inherent behavioral code an organism lives by. Natural government is everywhere, for every organism on Earth displays its own government. Each has its own "proper" or "desired" pattern of behavior. Furthermore, a human being has natural government. A person living alone in Nature has his own rules to live by. He has an established collection of behavioral precepts by which he conducts his daily life. His system may be well-planned in design or it may be fairly spontaneous. Regardless of the amount of detail it entails, it is in place.

As we know, throughout the world the species of organisms vary in structural and functional complexity. They vary in the developmental status of their brain and therefore they differ in their conception of rational behavior. Because of this, species vary in their respective level of natural government. The natural government of man is involved as a human being is a highly complex organism. Man's natural government is based on attributes from both his physiological and psychological self. On the biological side, natural government is greatly influenced by instinct and affected by how an individual functions within an ecosystem to meet his biological needs. On the non-biological side, it's influenced by the cultural environment. Like many aspects of human nature, it's modified by social conditioning and tempered by man through his use of reason.

The natural government of man is founded on a set of beliefs which reflect one's fundamental values and ideals. The basis for what a person believes is derived from what he learns from his parents, teachers, and others. The beliefs are inherently entwined with a sense of religious conviction. To a large extent, natural government represents a moral order that man perceives is both helpful and desirable to live by.

How does natural government work? From day to day, everyone determines how he's going to live. Everyone makes decisions on current endeavors as well as on long-term goals. For example, a person determines if he'll plow the fields so he can plant grain crops. He decides if he is going to slaughter a cow in order to feed his family. He decides if he is going to help his neighbor build a barn. He decides whether or not he'll go into town to purchase clothing.

Similarly, a person decides if he is going to enroll in a college to secure a better education, or if he's going to enlist in the military to serve his country. He determines whether or not he'll move to another city in search of a higher paying job. He decides if he should save money in order to purchase a new house. He determines when it's time to buy new furniture and when its time to trade in his automobile. Examples such as these represent situations in life where one is called upon to exercise his freedom of natural government.

Overall, the natural government of man reflects several basic characteristics of human nature. One of these characteristics is reasonableness. A human being is a rational organism and he uses reason to plan activities and monitor behavior. Another characteristic is cohesiveness. A human being desires a secure life, and to that end, he's organized and approaches problems in a methodical manner. He prefers to know ahead of time the consequences of his actions. Another characteristic is fairness. For the most part, a human being is open and honest. He desires justice and wants equal rights and opportunities in everyday life. Another characteristic is gregariousness. A human being is a socially-orientated organism. For him, interactions with other people are desirable and he enjoys friendships and shared experiences. Further, he desires interactions which are satisfying and beneficial. Such interactions may include helping a neighbor paint his house, or offering a relative a place to stay when he's out or work and moves into town. Another characteristic is morality. A human being is a moral creature who sets standards for himself and behaves in a manner that he expects others to emulate. These attributes, as well as others, form the basis for the natural government of man.

In many respects, human government represents nothing more than correct human behavior. Throughout history, in an attempt to achieve correct behavior, mankind has set forth rules to instruct him on how to live. The sources of the rules are many. For instance, there are religious rules like the Ten Commandments. There are social rules written into law and there are the unwritten rules held by custom and tradition. The social rules written into law are the rules of government and they form the guiding principles of institutionalized government.

Institutional government issues forth from natural government. It transfers control of human behavior on important issues from the individual person to society as a whole. Institutional government develops as a political association of people who are committed to establishing order in society. Institutional government's role is to establish equitable human interaction, tempered with reason, as the sanctioned form of social behavior.

The formation of institutional government brings stability to people's lives. It creates an established authority in society, and once in place, everyone becomes accountable for his or her behavior. For the most part, an institutional government is structured into distinct administrative sectors based on the particular functions they perform. The sectors include a legislative group, a police or military force, an executive bureaucracy, and a system of courts.

The foundation of institutional government lies in law, wherein the major responsibility of institutional government is to draft and enforce the laws of the land. The laws define the conditions for proper human conduct and establish the criteria needed to judge human behavior as either appropriate or inappropriate. Laws sanction secular legal authority. The laws determine the activities which are beneficial or unbeneficial to social progress. The established laws encourage people to follow mutually supported rules of acceptable human behavior.

Where do the laws of man issue forth from? A majority of the laws are social laws. For the most part, the rules influencing everyday behavior are not written down into a formal doctrine. The expectation that people are polite and friendly when they interact with one another is an example. Another example is the understanding that if you come upon a person who's injured, say in an auto accident, you stop and attempt to help him or her to the best of your ability. Such laws, i.e., directives of acceptable social behavior, are founded on tradition and develop through custom and usage. They're based upon the mutual acceptance of people who live together in a common socio-economic environment. The social laws are passed from one generation to the next and follow along the traditions of family units, neighborhood groups, and community associations.

The laws of institutional government, on the other hand, are documented. Government laws are officially sanctioned by the nation's controlling secular authority. Like the unwritten social laws, the laws of government are based on acceptable forms of human behavior. National governments establish laws that are designed to protect citizens from personal and economic harm. An example is the implementation of highway speed limits by municipalities in order to promote automobile safety. Another example is declaring the possession and distribution of illegal drugs a crime, thereby attempting to maintain and protect overall community health. The legislative branches of government draw up laws to establish a social atmosphere promoting safety, equality, and morality. The executive bureaus are structured to administer the laws. The police agencies are authorized to enforce the laws; and the courts, in turn, are in place to dole out fair and equitable resolutions to human conflict according to the laws.

We should mention that religious laws, like the laws of government, are laid down in doctrine. Religious doctrine defines proper behavior relative to principles, which in the believer's eyes are fundamental to and have acceptance of the deity. An example is the requirement for Muslims to pray five times a day in veneration of Allah. Another example is the acceptance of the Ten Commandments as guiding principles of the Judeo-Christian religion. The religious laws are highly moralistic. They instruct people on proper behavior as it pertains to living a life of not causing harm to others.

They further promote the well-being of others in regard to their physical, emotional, and spiritual health. Although similar in content, the religious and governmental laws are administered separately. In most societies the religious laws aren't enforced through police agencies and court decrees. Unless governments are controlled by religious authorities, religious laws are enforced by an acceptance of faith and a personal sense of duty.

All of the laws of mankind are a product of an extensive and complex evolution of human culture. These include the unwritten social laws, the laws of institutional governments, and the laws of religious doctrine. Cultural development finds its basis in our innate outlook on life. It is a rational and moralistic outlook. It is founded in man's biological evolution and derived from the development of the human psychological self.

All institutional governments work to meet the legal needs of society. All institutional governments draft laws to regulate civil and criminal behavior. Whether in the business arena, the marketplace, or the town square, the citizens must be protected. Human rights must be defined and guaranteed. All world governments establish bureaucracies to administer the approved laws. Some governments invest all of the power within a single body. This is the case for a monarchy. Others divide the responsibilities among separate and equivalent branches of government. This occurs with the governments that favor a democracy.

Those governments which divide up responsibilities usually consist of two or three independent branches. The three-branched governments consist of legislative, executive, and judicative sectors. Each has specific functions in regard to the application of law. The legislative branch drafts the laws. The legislative sector has the responsibility to write the laws, approve them, and institute them as officially binding. The executive branch is made up of bureaucratic and policing agencies. The executive branch administers and enforces the laws. In this respect, the executive sector has the responsibility to apprehend those individuals who break the laws. The judicial branch of government is charged with the proper application of the laws. It is concerned with justice under the laws. The judicial branch is composed of civil and criminal courts and it presides over disputes which involve individuals, organizations, and other entities of society. The judicial sector utilizes a process of jury and trial to determine if individuals adhere to the law. Additionally, the judicial sector's role is to interpret legality and determine which laws are valid and which are not.

Institutional governments provide a number of important functions to society. One of these functions is to guarantee people with certain rights and freedoms. This includes the right to vote, the right to own property, the right to a trial by one's peers, etc.

Another function is to prevent illegal activities. A government upholds the laws through control of the criminal element of society. It apprehends and punishes those individuals who break the laws. To do so, it maintains a police force.

Another function of government is to maintain order when it comes to civil matters. That is, a government settles disagreements between competing members of society. It could involve citizens, as occurs in a dispute over the property line between two neighbors. It might involve businesses, as takes place in a disagreement between two companies over the manufacturing rights to a specific product.

Institutional government further sets standards in regard to public safety. It monitors the condition of the workplace to eliminate potential health hazards. It determines the criteria for the reliability and performance of manufactured products. It also sets limits on the permissible degree of soil, water, and air pollution. In general, government works to maintain a safe and healthy environment throughout the entire social structure.

Another function of government is to guard against economic infringement. Institutional government regulates the monetary system of a nation. Likewise, it establishes tariffs and sets quotas on foreign imports. It also puts safeguards in place to prevent private corporations from monopolizing goods and services.

Another important function of institutional government is to protect the citizens from hostile aggression, whether arising from within or without the country. That is, it maintains a national militia to protect against internal rebellion. Likewise, government maintains an army and navy to protect its people from outside aggression.

Finally, another function of institutional government is to represent the citizenry in foreign affairs. A country's government forms alliances and enters into treaties with other nations.

In addition to meeting the above functions, institutional government provides a number of important services to the people who live under its jurisdiction. For example, it builds and maintains highways. It operates the public school system. It provides food and housing allowances and other welfare benefits to its citizens. Institutional government establishes and maintains major health care programs as well. It usually owns and operates the postal system. Institutional government may or may not own and operate the communication and transportation networks. It may or may not own and distribute the energy and utility supplies. Finally, institutional government makes available to the citizens certain recreational facilities. For example, it sets land aside for public parks and wildlife refuges.

There are considerable benefits to living under the jurisdiction of an institutionalized government. Citizens are entitled to many guarantees and amenities offered by their government. As we said, the citizens are entitled to equal rights and equal protection under the law. The citizens are also entitled to equal services provided by government including education, welfare, and health care.

In order to receive the benefits of government, there are certain obligations on the part of the citizens. The people are required to uphold their system of government. They do so in several ways. People support government by obeying its laws. They support government by providing revenues which are secured through taxation. The people support government through obligatory duty such as service in the armed forces. Further, the citizens take part in the sanctioned political and legal endeavors occurring in their nation. First and foremost, they vote in local, provincial, and national elections. Additionally, they serve on jury duty. People also support government through their participation in local community organizations. For example, they provide volunteer service to the neighborhood ambulance and fire departments. Finally, the people support government through allegiance. They hold and display a strong sense of loyalty to the type of government under which they live.

All institutional governments attempt to maintain a social environment which allows the citizens to meet their needs. We know that human beings are identical the world over and their basic needs remain the same. Similarly, the responsibilities people hold are the same regardless of the government or social structure under which they live. And across the world, governments and citizens face the same challenges over and over again.

Let's discuss a major charge of institutional government. As noted, one of the most important responsibilities institutional government has is to control the criminal element of society. We're well aware that all the social turmoil in the world is the result of crime. Assault, kidnap, rape, and murder are acts of crime. Beating and maiming are acts of crime. Arson, robbery, embezzlement, and theft are acts of crime. One of the major designs of any government is to apprehend the individuals who commit crime. It's the role of institutional government to punish the people who break the law.

Acts of crime are widespread, and we know there are many reasons why people attempt to injure others. Physical harm takes place because of hatred. Harm occurs because of misunderstanding and jealously. Harm comes about because of prejudice, which may be due to differences of ethnicity and race. It comes about because of the differences people hold in their political and religious beliefs, greed for another's wealth or property, and simply because of the desire to injure or maim someone. There are many reasons why crime takes place. For whatever reasons, it permeates every society and disrupts the fabric of constructive social living.

Currently there are several types of government in the world and each type must address the issue of crime. Whatever the basis for a particular government, it must provide an environment for the peaceful conduct of daily life. In regards to the administration of justice, it's important to state that the designated punishment should equate to the severity of the crime. Crimes range from premeditated murder to shop lifting. The punishments range from capital punishment and life imprisonment to yearly, monthly, and daily sentences. There should be set limits of jail time established for specific crimes such as armed robbery, battery, rape, manslaughter, etc. Rather than be offered an abbreviated sentence prior to trial and conviction, each accused person should be required to face, in a fair jurisprudence process, the full consequences of his or her actions. Rather than be awarded time off for good behavior once imprisoned, each criminal who has been tried by jury and declared guilty should be required to serve the length of his or her initial sentence. During the time served, each convicted criminal should be required to work in a prison-based occupation which produces a product or provides a service of benefit to humanity. During incarceration, each convicted criminal forfeits certain societal rights such as the right to vote, the right to pursue economic gain, the right to participate in public forums, etc. Also, while incarcerated, each convicted criminal shouldn't be awarded additional benefits, such as granted leaves away from prison or unsupervised congenial visits by family and friends, etc. Thus, every government has the responsibility to control the criminal element in society. Every government must protect the people who adhere to its laws and punish those who do not.

At this point, let's restate some key benefits of institutional governments. Governments maintain law and order. They establish and guarantee civil liberties. Governments promote equitable employment conditions in business and industry so people can earn an adequate living. Governments further allow for the establishment of mass transportation and communication networks. Governments provide an opportunity to the equitable procurement of basic human necessities as well. The access to food, clothing, and housing are facilitated and promoted by government. Likewise, education and health care availabilities are promoted by government to the citizens of society. These benefits represent several of the contributions institutional governments make towards the advancement of social living.

Additional to these benefits, the most significant endorsement made by institutional government relevant to social living is acceptance of the principle of the equality of all human beings. To a large extent, the basis of modern day government rests upon this premise. The concept relating to "all men are created equal" is fundamental to the constitutions of numerous governments. The constitutions of nations worldwide demand that equal rights be available to all people regardless of differences in age, sex, race, or ethnic background. Many societies have progressed to the point where the practice of equality among the citizens of a nation is vital to their pursuit of happiness. This is an important concept for the human species, and it serves as a prelude to eventual acceptance of the fact that in God's eyes all creatures of life are created equal.

Like all social institutions, the institution of government has undergone considerable modification. In the early years, government took the form of political power vested in a singular authority. One or more powerful leaders made all the important social, economic, and military decisions for affined groups of people living together. After thousands of years, autocratic rule gave way to more representative forms of decision-making. From the initial stages of authoritative and tribal control, institutional government developed into the highly structured political systems of the twenty-first century.

Today, there are several different types of institutional governments in the world. The various types are utilized by over seven billion people who are politically divided into some two hundred nations. Basically, the world's governments fall into one of two broad categories. These two categories are the representative democracy and the authoritative-totalitarian form of government. Each type administers to the legal needs of society. Each maintains a legislative component whose role is to draft the laws. Each type establishes an executive bureaucracy and a system of courts to enforce the laws.

The democratic and totalitarian types of government differ from one another in several important aspects however. Foremost, they differ in regard to the way political power is delegated. They also differ in the number of liberties their citizens enjoy. The two types of government further differ in how economic wealth is distributed across the various societal factions. The governments differ as to who owns and operates the major industrial and agricultural complexes as well. The governments differ as to who controls key forces of energy, transportation, communication, etc. Finally, the two types differ as to what extent government interacts, or interferes, with the other institutions of society such as family and religion.

The totalitarian forms of government include the monarchies, oligarchies, theocracies, and dictatorships. Totalitarian governments are ruled by a single authority, whether it consists of one person or a group of politically aligned individuals. The "right to rule" is based on one of several non-democratic avenues: i.e., inheritance vis-a-vis a member of a royal family, an established tribal hierarchy, a sanctioned religious order, or by means of despotic control that's supported by a strong military or police force.

Traditionally, the authoritative governments afford the least amount of individual liberties. These governments usually limit basic human rights such as the right to vote, the right to own property, the right to express oneself freely. Totalitarian governments control the major economic forces in society. They control sources of energy as well as the resources for manufacturing. Further, totalitarian governments establish production quotas and usually own all the significant businesses and industries. They operate the nation's transportation and communication networks as well. Past examples of authoritative-totalitarian governments include the kingships of England, France and Spain during the fifteenth and sixteenth centuries, and the tribal leaderships of the American Indians of the seventeenth, eighteenth, and nineteenth centuries. Current examples of countries with highly authoritative rule include the kingdoms of Swaziland and Saudi Arabia, as well as the centralistic regimes of North Korea and Cuba.

The governments that provide the most liberties to the citizens are the representative democracies. Representative democracies are ruled by officials chosen by the citizens through an "open" elective process. The eligibility of officials and the term lengths they serve are determined on a nation-by-nation basis. So too is the size of the governing body relative to a country's overall population. Also determined on a nation-by-nation basis are the electoral process and the demographic make-up of the eligible electorate.

Countries with representative governments usually have economic structures that are either capitalistic or socialistic in nature. The representative governments with a capitalistic or profit-motivated bias usually promote free enterprise as the means for economic and industrial growth. Such governments are exemplified by the representative democracies of the United States, Canada, Australia, and the Confederation of Switzerland.

The representative governments with a socialistic slant often provide major health, educational, and welfare benefits to the people. In general, these governments provide less opportunity for private ownership and free enterprise than do capitalistic-biased governments. Typically the socialistic-based, representative governments have control over key economic forces and the major infrastructural units of society. That is, they usually operate the nation's communication network as well as its transportation system. They often maintain operational control over the large manufacturing complexes like the steel industry. Likewise, they either own or tightly control the utilities of gas, oil, and coal, as well as the nuclear power industry. Recent examples of nations whose governments place high emphasis on socialistic-based, economic programs include India, France, Norway, and the Netherlands.

People the world over are concerned with the amount of power a particular form of government wields. An inherent problem of any type of government is that it may be too restrictive. The government might exert too much control and demand too many obligations from its people. Such would be the case of an authoritative-totalitarian government where individual freedoms are often abridged. A similar situation takes place when the citizens voluntarily surrender too much control to government. This is likely to happen with a representative democracy that oversees a socialistic-focused economic system. Such governments tend to receive more power than necessary, as the citizens often relinquish a number of personal responsibilities. The citizens surrender authority since they expect government to provide all major services including child care, education, medical coverage, and retirement provisions for the elderly. Typically, the people within a socialistic-based system expect the government to provide complete care from the cradle to grave. The representative democracy, based on a free-enterprise or capitalistic economic structure, generally allows its citizenry to retain a greater degree of control over socio-economic forces than either the socialistic representative or totalitarian form of government.

For the most part, the representative type of government, whether socialistic or capitalistic centered, isn't overly restrictive for it grants numerous rights and liberties to the citizens. Likewise, the representative democracy attempts to provide basic services in regard to education, health care, and welfare. Unlike the totalitarian type, however, it generally doesn't own and operate the major economic elements of society.

Neither of the two major forms of governments, totalitarian or representative democracy, is free from economic discrimination. Under both forms of government, the political forces are often aligned such that the rich get wealthier and the poor become more destitute. For example, the totalitarian governments control wealth through decree based on autocratic decision-making. The representative democracy, with a socialistic emphasis, controls wealth by way of the establishment of an elaborate bureaucratic infrastructure. The representative, free-enterprise government, in turn, provides a biased incentive-based network to individuals and corporations as the means to monitor wealth. An example of an economic incentive is the tax breaks given to certain businesses to conduct their operations in a given locale. Another example is the easing of safety standards to various energy providers relative to the production and distribution of energy supplies. Such incentives are intended to promote industrial growth throughout the private sector of society. Although unfortunate, the opportunity for economic discrimination takes place under all types of institutional government.

Regardless of the form of government, inconsistency and unfairness can arise when it involves protecting the rights of citizens and providing for their welfare. Oftentimes, we see hypocrisy in the leaders of nations when it comes to making decisions on issues involving the support of hostilities vs. peaceful negotiation, issues concerning economic gain vs. environmental endangerment, and issues dealing with the distribution of revenues for domestic programs vs. foreign aid. At times, the keepers of government place their personal or partisan interests above the general good.

Under most circumstances, governments must reach a compromise across the socio-economic and political arenas. That is, on the individual citizen's level, the institutional governments must guarantee fundamental liberties and rights. On a broader scale, governments cannot become overly restrictive towards business and industry by way of more regulations or higher taxes, which can hinder product development and opportunities for expanded trade. Rather, governments must remain the keepers of justice for everyone. A key charge for institutional government then is to continually choose between what's right for the individual citizen versus what's best for society as a whole.

Knowing the basis for government and considering the two general types cited above, how should a universal government be structured? Would it be totalitarian and restrictive in nature, or would it be a representative form and advance democratic principles? Instead of either of these, should the universal government of mankind be something else? Should it be highly focused on the natural government of man? Or, should it reflect a composite of several modern-day national governments?

The universal government ought to look like the following. From a practical standpoint, the universal government of mankind should be a representative democracy. It should be designed so the collective inputs of average citizens have control over the economic and political forces of society. A representative democracy would provide the greatest opportunity of participation for the vast majority of people. It would give the citizens an equal voice via their right to vote. It would provide the citizens with a set of common privileges and rights. Further, it would offer the people equal protection under the law and a uniform justice system with trial by jury.

How should the universal institution of government be structured and what branches would it contain? The universal institution of government would consist of three branches, the legislative, executive, and judicial branches of government. In many respects, it would be structured similar to the government of the United States of America.

The legislative branch will consist of two houses or divisions. All of the legislative members shall be elected directly by the people. One house will consist of representatives chosen to promote and protect the interests of the individual citizen. The other house will consist of representatives chosen to express and vote the interests of the population as a whole.

In chapter 2, we discussed the reasons why people left the independent state of Nature to form societies. We talked about the political beliefs of Locke and Rousseau. In this chapter, we focus on both natural and institutional government and the role they play in influencing the design of a universal government and the cultural development of man. Historically, natural government is the government of the individual person.

Institutional government, on the other hand, is the government of society as a whole. The two divisions of the legislative branch of government ought to reflect these separate and distinct interests.

Each legislative house will have the same number of representatives. The representatives to the two houses shall be selected on a regional basis from across the nation. A region will be determined by population and adjusted on a preset timetable according to demographic shifts in the population. For each house, the number of representatives shall be proportional to the number of citizens who live within the specified region. Note that the members of the legislature will not represent regional political interests per se. There's no need for a universal government to be structured with its members selected for the purpose of representing the interests of a province, a county, or a state within the nation. Rather, the reason for electing one representative over another to the house that promotes "individual liberties" is because a majority of voters believe a certain candidate would better serve the interests of the average citizen. Likewise, the reason to elect a particular candidate to the house which supports the "general citizenry" is due to the fact the voters think that candidate would better advance the overall goals of society. Hence, the basis for representation ought to be issue driven rather than dependent upon geographical territory.

The legislative branch of government shall have the power to make all laws. The legislative branch will evaluate the actions of individuals, associations, organizations, and corporations within society. It will determine what activities are to be sanctioned as fair and acceptable behavior. Based on these determinations, the legislative branch shall draft ordinances and rules. It will then enact these rules into law. To be enacted into law, the drafted regulations must first be approved by each house of the legislature.

The legislative branch has several additional functions to perform. For one, it shall establish the nation's medium of exchange. It will coin money and determine its value. The legislative branch shall also determine the need for taxes and levy them. This includes income, property, and sales taxes. It also includes subsistence, education, health care, and recreation taxes. The legislative branch will collect the taxes it levies as well as impose and collect additional sources of income such as tariffs, tolls, licenses, and other fees. Based on societal needs, and in concurrence with other major institutions of society, it will determine how the incoming revenues are to be distributed.

The legislative branch shall regulate commerce. It will monitor the buying, selling, and trading of commodities. Similarly, it will regulate the distribution of such commodities, either within the nation proper or with foreign countries.

The legislative branch shall work with the various institutions of society to establish standards throughout the nation. For example, relative to the institution of employment, it will determine the performance criteria for manufactured products and set conditions regarding their distribution. Also, it will set guidelines for the proper administration of various service jobs throughout the nation.

Reflective of the established, operating principles of other institutions, the legislative branch shall establish additional standards. For example, the legislature will set performance standards in education, which means it'll determine the criteria which constitute the requirements for a well-rounded elementary and high school education. In addition, the legislative branch will establish the standards for quality medical and health care. It will also determine the regulations for a safe work environment. It will set the codes on the construction of houses and buildings. The legislative branch shall decide other health and safety issues as well. For example, it will determine the minimum nutritional content required in processed food. It will determine the ecological requirements for a non-polluted environment and set limits on the emissions from automobiles, trucks, and airplanes, as well as power plants and other industrial sites. Finally, the legislative branch will determine other units of conformity within society such as the standard for weights and measures.

Further, the legislative branch of government shall determine the requirements for citizenship.

The executive branch of the universal government shall consist of a bureaucracy of public officials and civil servants. It will contain a network of police agencies, detention centers, and various penal facilities. Additionally, it will contain the militia and armed forces. The executive branch shall be headed by a president and two vice presidents. The president will have overall responsibility for the executive branch of government. One vice president will be in charge of domestic programs while the other vice president will be in charge of foreign affairs.

There shall be two cabinet-level administrative boards. One board shall consist of ministers and their assistants. This board's responsibility will be to interact with the several major institutions of society, which are described in chapters 3 through 8. Each minister shall head a liaison office that interfaces with a major institution. The liaison office's duties are twofold. The first is to ensure the institution operates within the constraints of the law. The second is to promote and facilitate the institution's performance towards the betterment of social living. There shall be a minister of Family, Religion, Employment, Education, Health, Recreation, Communication, Transportation, Financial Resource, Utility-Service, Energy, Ecology, Environment, and Discovery. The other board in the executive branch shall consist of directors and their assistants. The second board's function is to oversee the various governmental departments. There shall be a Department of Police, Militia, Military (Defense), Taxation, Treasury, Postal Services, Commerce, Foreign Relations (State), Basic Support (Welfare), Relief (Emergency), and Standards (Life-Quality). Each department shall administer its duties and responsibilities for the nation's citizens as determined by law.

The president, vice presidents, boards of ministers and directors, and the heads of police, militia, and military shall be elected directly by the people. These administrators will hold office for specified terms of service.

The executive branch of government shall have the responsibility to enforce all laws approved by the legislative branch.

The executive branch shall provide citizens with protection from civil and criminal violations of their rights. The executive branch will establish a police force to enforce the laws. It will maintain the detention centers, jails, and prisons for the incarceration of people convicted of civil misconduct as well as criminal behavior.

The executive branch shall establish a militia to protect the citizens from internal rebellion. It will provide arms, equipment, quarters, and monetary support for the militia.

The executive branch shall establish armed forces to protect the citizens from aggression by foreign adversaries. The executive branch will maintain an army, navy, and air force. It will provide arms, quarters, and all other necessary support for the armed forces.

The executive branch of government shall have the power to draw up treaties with foreign nations. It will appoint diplomatic representatives and receive ambassadors from other countries.

The executive branch shall have the authority to declare war with concurrence from the legislative and judicial branches.

The executive branch of government shall establish a civil defense network to aid citizens during periods of disaster. The civil defense network will maintain a national protective agency to provide support during catastrophic events such as floods, hurricanes, earthquakes, and nuclear power plant accidents. The civil defense network will maintain a national ambulance service to provide citizens with emergency medical treatment. It will also maintain a national fire department to combat fires in public buildings and government facilities, as well as in national forests and parklands.

The judicial branch of the universal government shall consist of a network of courts established to administer justice under the law. The court system shall be comprised of two major divisions, which are civil law and criminal law. There will be courts to settle civil disputes and separate courts to try criminal cases. Each division will be structured into minor, inferior, superior, and supreme levels. Each division will have an established appellate process in place. Each division will administer justice through use of the trial process whereby citizen juries will be called together to pass judgments and render verdicts. The judges shall determine and apply the appropriate level of punishment, or compensation, as defined by the specifications of law.

The judicial branch shall consist of a hierarchy of courts. As indicated, there will be a civil court division and a criminal court division. Within each, there will be a distribution of responsibilities with sectors from both court systems specialized according to subject matter. For example, in the civil court network there will be a section that oversees violations of civil rights including property right disputes, contract infringements, etc. Within the criminal court network, there will be a section that oversees crimes such as fraud and embezzlement, as well as a section that oversees bodily harm violations such as rape, stabbings, shootings, etc. For both the civil and criminal systems, there will be an appellate process in place whereby the upper courts will review decisions of lower courts within their specified areas of jurisdiction.

The judicial system shall be further structured to the extent that disputes among individual people will be settled in courts which focus on citizen-related issues. For example, it will contain courts that deal with family-related matters and include the resolution of problems involving children, juveniles, and adults. The disputes among businesses, on the other hand, will be settled in corporation-focused courts. It will deal with issues that involve organizations, associations, and corporations. For instance, the judicial branch dealing with corporations, etc., shall contain a subdivision or section dedicated to resolve manufacturing disputes. Likewise, it shall contain a section that deals with disputes arising from the buying, selling, and trading of goods and services. It shall also contain a section to handle transportation and communication matters. Further, it shall contain a section to address consumer health and safety concerns.

The judicial branch of government shall have the jurisdiction to settle all disputes and transgressions. It will interpret the law and determine whether the law is being upheld or breached. The judicial branch will determine the level of benefit, reward, or exoneration for individuals, groups, and organizations that are the recipients of a favorable judgment of a court proceeding. Likewise, the judicial branch will determine the level of loss, penalty, or punishment for individuals, groups, and organizations that are the recipients of an unfavorable judgment. The judicial branch of government will determine all levels of monetary fines. Similarly, it will determine all degrees of physical labor that's to be assigned as punishment. It will determine all lengths of time for incarceration in jail or prison. It will also have the power to order capital punishment. Finally, the judicial branch of government shall have the authority to grant pardons and reprieves.

We've thus described the structure of a universal institution of government. Once established, it has one overriding role in society. That role is to protect the other institutions so they can function and meet their duties in a responsible manner. The institution of government should regulate the other institutions to the extent these institutions don't infringe upon one another, nor abuse their individual powers. Similarly, it should regulate other institutions to the extent they don't interfere with the people's ability to pursue their purpose in life. Additionally, the universal institution of government has a number of responsibilities it owes the citizens. It must guarantee basic rights such as the right to vote, own property, bear arms, etc. It must offer certain safeguards such as the protection from the criminal elements of society. Further, it must provide its own services including the establishment of in-house communication and transportation networks that allow the citizens to effectively interface with government. Such services would also enable the government to meet its operational needs. Finally, the universal institution of government requires specific obligations from the citizens. It must receive support and a measurable level of service from the people who live under its jurisdiction.

The universal institution of government must guarantee the following rights to its citizens. It must guarantee the right to have equal opportunity under the law. It must guarantee freedom, liberty, and the opportunity for the pursuit of happiness.

The universal institution of government must guarantee the right for equal opportunity to housing, clothing, subsistence (food), health care, education, employment, utilities, transportation, communication, and recreation. It must also guarantee the freedom of religion and the freedom of political views. Likewise, the universal institution of government should guarantee freedom of speech and freedom of the press. It should guarantee the right for peaceful assembly. Further, it should guarantee the right to entreat and petition the government over grievances.

The universal institution of government must guarantee the right to pursue retribution through legal proceedings for damage to property or self. In conjunction with this, it needs to guarantee its citizens due process under the law. For instance, if charged with a crime each person is entitled to direct knowledge of the civil or criminal charges placed against him. Likewise, each person is entitled to an immediate and fair trial. The trial should be public and the jury should consist of one's peers. To the extent possible, the jurors should be unbiased and open to varying opinions. Witnesses should be allowed to testify either in support of, or against, the accused individual.

The universal institution of government must not allow dangerous health and safety situations to exist in society. That is, it should offer protection against unsafe labor conditions in the workplace. The universal institution of government must ensure safety in the production, distribution, and utilization of manufactured products. It should ensure that housing is structurally sound with protective measures established relative to wind, fire, flood, and earthquake damage. It should offer protection against unsafe utility situations in regard to the production, refinement, and distribution of energy resources. It should offer protection against unsafe conditions in the fields of communication and transportation as well. The universal institution of government should ensure that all processed foods meet requirements for nutritional quality. Similarly, it should ensure safety in the provision of human services and health care. It should ensure that medicines are effective and non-harmful as prescribed. Likewise, it should offer protection against unsafe environmental conditions. That is, it ought to provide protection against water impurity, soil contamination, and air pollution. Finally, the universal institution of government should offer protection against unsafe situations which arise in the areas of recreation and sports.

The universal institution of government must provide protection against social bias or discrimination based on age, sex, race, ethnic background, political views, religion, etc. Further, it should offer protection against unreasonable search and detainment by police agencies. It should also provide for the safeguard of an individual's rights during arrest and trial. It should provide protection against unreasonable monetary or property fines. It should ensure the protection against intimidation, aggression, or torture as forms of punishment. Ultimately, the universal institution of government should ensure criminals are apprehended and appropriately punished. Accordingly, it should put in place fixed terms of incarceration that prevent convicted criminals from having early release from prison with an opportunity to recommit crimes against society.

Additionally, the universal institution of government ought to provide the following safeguards to society. As discussed, it should protect the citizens from aggression and physical harm. It should establish a police agency to guard against the criminal element of society. It should establish a national militia to deter internal rebellion as well as a military force to defend against outside aggression.

The universal institution of government should offer the following services to its citizens. It should provide a postal system by which it can interface with other institutions and the citizenry at large. This post office would be utilized for government business only, whereas the nation's general postal duties would be handled through mail delivery services housed within the institution of communication. The institution of government should coin money and ensure a sound system of monetary exchange. Also, it should provide public parklands, forests, lakes, and wildlife areas. And as needed, it should provide emergency relief for victims of natural disasters such as forest fires, floods, hurricanes, and earthquakes.

Regarding the operations of other institutions in society, the universal institution of government should ensure conditions exist so the following human requisites and services are provided. It should ensure that a national education system can be established. It should ensure national transportation and communication networks can be put in place. It must ensure that basic health care can be made available to the nation's citizenry. It must also ensure conditions exist in society so housing, clothing, and subsistence (food) can be provided to all people who don't have the means to support themselves, i.e., those who are physically handicapped, mentally challenged, destitute, impoverished, etc. Overall, the universal institution of government must maintain an environment conducive to the other institutions so they can successfully meet their designated duties and responsibilities.

Finally, as mentioned, the universal institution of government ought to require the following obligations on the part of the citizens. The government should be supported through adherence to the laws of the land, taxation, and voluntary service in one of the branches of government or in any of the major societal institutions.

Citizens ought to volunteer for civil service in the legislative, executive, and judicial branches of government. Citizens should volunteer for service in the police, militia, or armed forces. Also, people should volunteer for service in hospitals, post offices, national parks, and wildlife areas. They should volunteer for service in schools, libraries, museums, and other educational centers. Citizens ought to volunteer for service in organizations that support the poor, impoverished, physically and mentally ill, physically handicapped, etc. Likewise, the citizens should volunteer to serve in agencies that provide assistance to the victims of natural disasters. Thus, to ensure the well-being of society, the universal institution of government should expect its citizens to provide a significant level of allegiance and support.

Although it's only one of several institutions of mankind, government is a most important one. It is most important because its main function is to preserve and protect the other institutions of society. Government is the pituitary institution of social anatomy. It is the center about which nearly all of the other institutions revolve.

The universal institution of government would likely be called upon to raise revenues for the operations of other institutions such as communication, transportation, and so forth. However, it wouldn't exercise control over these institutions by manipulating their purse strings. Rather, government is the conduit for raising revenues through taxation and other means, but only if the other institutions are unable to secure sufficient revenues on their own. Whatever revenues government does provide, it turns the monies over to the institutions' boards of directors which have control over how the funds are distributed.

We should point out regarding the several societal institutions, government wouldn't be called upon to raise revenues to support the institution of religion. Based on the principle of separation of church and state, religion would secure its own resources, financial and otherwise.

Government should neither administer nor coordinate the operations of any other institution of society. For example, it wouldn't determine a religion's hierarchy or its rules of operation. Instead, the universal government's role is to protect the establishment of the other institutions of society, such as the institution of religion. Thus, government should protect religion and ensure its fundamental right to exist as a social institution.

The primary function of a universal government then is to provide an environment for the peaceful conduct of life. Government's main responsibility is to establish and maintain conditions in society which allow man to pursue his purpose in life through the several institutions of family, church, employment, etc. Government enables the various entities of society to practice human rights on a daily basis. It has control over the legal components and provides for equal rights and opportunities. It also has control over the commercial components and provides for the equitable transfer of goods and services. Further, government establishes law and order. As the controlling element of society, it provides security and stability. In return, government requires the fulfillment of specific obligations from its citizens.

We might ask, what's the overriding value of a universal government for mankind? The answer is that a universal government offers an atmosphere for the peaceful conduct of social living. It would provide a place, i.e., a country or perhaps an entire planet. And it would provide a time, that is, several centuries or possibly several-hundred thousand centuries. Thus, a universal government would guarantee conditions prevail in the world by which mankind can live in a stable, social environment and exercise his call to life.

In order to pursue his purpose in life, mankind must have a government that is "right". To become the gardener and governor of Nature, man must have a government that is "proper". To promote and preserve the welfare of himself and the other creatures around him, mankind must have a government that is "correct".

But what is "right", "proper", and "correct" government? And who decides it? The answer is: we do! The people of the world decide it. Once "correct" government is defined, it should become the basis for the universal government of mankind.

Politicians have discussed the role of government in society for centuries. Marcus Cicero was a Roman statesman who had specific thoughts on "correct" government. Cicero identified a moral relationship between the human experience and the deity in which aspects of this relationship were manifested in society as justice, and as such, were applied by man through the use of reason. According to Cicero, "Moreover, virtue exists in man and God alike, . . . virtue, however, is nothing else than Nature perfected and developed to its highest point; therefore there is a likeness between man and God."[1] "For those creatures who have received the gift of reason from Nature have also received right reason, and therefore they have also received the gift of Law, which is right reason applied to command and prohibition. And if they have received Law, they have received Justice also."[2] Cicero likewise stated " . . . the first common possession of man and God is reason. But those who have reason in common must also have right reason in common. And since right reason is Law . . ."[3]

Throughout history, mankind has been taught what "correct" government ought to be. The people of today's world know the value of enlightenment over ignorance. They know the value of opportunity over non-opportunity and of freedom over slavery. They know the value of equality over inequality as well as the value of justice over injustice. Such key social precepts have been recognized by mankind for a long, long time. In order to have "correct" government, man must determine what's right. Then, man must always do what is right. This is the basis for the establishment and performance of a universal government.

It's not difficult for human beings to do what is right. Nonetheless, living in today's world is neither simple nor straightforward. Societal life is neither all good nor all bad. Societal life isn't 100 percent right or 100 percent wrong. There are extenuating circumstances to decision-making and choosing from competing options isn't easy. Indeed, at times it's difficult to decide between right and wrong. However, once a decision is made the execution of what's decided isn't difficult at all.

We then might ask who accepts the responsibility to decide what's right. Who accepts the responsibility to determine the best means to administer a government so the state will prosper and people will be secure? The responsibility lies with us. It lies with the people themselves. It's the responsibility of each individual citizen and the human race as a whole.

1. Sprague, E. and P. W. Taylor, *Knowledge and Value*, 1959, p. 606.
2. Ibid. p. 607.
3. Ibid. p. 605.

Whenever a human being finds it difficult to determine what is right, he only needs to remember this: do not intentionally harm others in physical or emotional ways. If still unsure, he should consult with God through prayer. Whenever human society finds it difficult to determine where justice lies, all it has to do is ask God. God will provide the answers. Mankind only needs to pray to God for guidance on what constitutes proper social behavior.

6

Social-Economic: Employment

PEOPLE HAVE ALWAYS HAD to find the means to earn a living and thereby obtain food, clothing, and shelter for themselves. The social-economic institution of employment provides the means for a person to earn a living. The employment structure provides the opportunity whereby a person can sustain himself and his dependents throughout his lifetime.

Most human beings spend a major portion of their adult life in an occupational role. A person works at a job to secure the resources needed to meet his biological needs. That is, he works to earn money so he can purchase food, clothing, shelter, medical supplies, etc. A person also works in order to satisfy his psychological needs. For instance, he works to acquire material goods which will make his life more enjoyable. He works to secure money so he can pursue recreational activities. Further, he works so he can accomplish new goals in life. Thus, the employment institution is designed to ensure all human needs are met. It's structured so the means to earn a living is available to anyone who is willing to work.

The employment structure provides several additional benefits to people. One benefit employment offers is the opportunity to identify oneself with a constructive cause. That is, a person can attain a sense of accomplishment when he works for a company that manufactures a product useful to society. Likewise, a person can gain a feeling of pride if he works for a business which provides an important service to mankind. Another benefit the employment structure offers is the recognition of social fulfillment. Employment brings people together in work-related activities, and as such, encourages interaction and co-operation. In industry, people work side-by-side to meet job production goals. They further interact with one another when they form unions to secure health care and other job-related benefits, such as higher pay rates for working overtime or holidays.

Another benefit the employment structure offers is to serve as an avenue for the expression of one's talents. Indeed, employment provides the means whereby a person can demonstrate his skills and creativity as it applies to the job. Another benefit of the employment structure is the overall promotion of a person's well-being. The very act of working requires an individual to exert himself physically and thereby helps to maintain one's health. Thus, the employment structure represents an important avenue for the expression of a person's assorted physical and mental attributes.

Within any social system, the employment structure shows a considerable level of diverseness. In modern times, the people in society work in a variety of occupational roles. They work at jobs in agriculture, commerce, business, and industry. They work at jobs in microbiology and space aeronautics. People also work in the fields of education, health care, communication, and transportation. The occupational role may be that of a teacher, factory worker, or cattle rancher. It may be a dentist, doctor, or lawyer. A person may be employed as a bus driver, airplane pilot, or truck driver. The job may be that of a bricklayer, carpenter, or electrician. It may be a salesperson or department store owner. Likewise, it may be a computer programmer or electrical engineer. Regardless of the type of the job, everyone is employed to support himself and his family. Regardless of the job's physical demands or intellectual requirements, everyone works to earn a living. And irrespective of the number of hours worked, everyone is employed in an occupation to sustain his day-to-day existence.

Throughout the world, there's substantial diversification to the institution of employment. The predominant means of earning a living varies greatly from one society to the next. There are social systems in which the employment structure is mainly agrarian. There, the majority of people work on farms. They tend to sheep and cattle, and produce the vegetables, fruits, and grain crops needed to support the members of their society. There are other societies which rely on the sea to sustain their way of life. Such social systems derive their livelihood from fishing and jobs related to the fishing industry. There are other societies which are heavily geared toward industrial development. For them, manufacturing forms the foundation of the employment structure. Their industries provide the majority of employment opportunities as they manufacture the products and goods needed to survive. Still other societies are dominated by jobs in forestry, mining, oil, and coal production. The social systems which favor these occupations employ people to secure and develop natural resources, which can then be bartered for useful and desirable commodities produced by workers in neighboring societies.

Not only does the institution of employment vary from society to society, but it differs from one generation to the next. The institution of employment has indeed undergone considerable change over the years. For instance, there are occupations today which didn't exist centuries ago. Some of these include the jobs of auto mechanic, school bus driver, and airplane pilot. Other "newer" jobs include those of telephone operator, television cameraman, and computer programmer. On the other hand, there are occupations that were fairly prevalent in past times but are no longer in vogue. Such occupations included the jobs of a village blacksmith, ice deliveryman, and chimneysweeper. Still other "obsolete" jobs include those of a covered wagon maker, frontier scout, and stagecoach driver.

Given the historical diversity to the institution of employment, we might ask what "component" serves as an underlying impetus to today's social-economic systems. That is, what causes the current systems to function the way they do? The component or fundamental mechanism which coordinates and drives the current social-economic systems is money. The quest to earn and spend money is the major driving force in a majority of societies throughout the world.

Money is used as the principal means of barter. It's the key to survival just as furs, livestock, or wampum was used in social systems of bygone times. It's the key to survival just as rice, wheat, or corn might be. It is a bargaining tool just as sources of fuel like coal, firewood, or oil would be. In today's world, money represents the prime medium of exchange used as a leverage to put goods and services on equitable, transferable grounds. Money is used as a measure of material worth, for it assigns a scale of value for goods and services. We further note that the precious metals of silver and gold are used as standards to identify and quantify monetary value.

As a result of working at their jobs in business and industry, people are able to earn money to purchase manufactured products. From working at their jobs people are able to secure services performed by other people. By working to produce goods, selling the goods to obtain money, and using the money to produce other goods and services, people maintain their social-economic well-being.

With the money they earn, people purchase the essential items they need such as food, clothing, and medicine. People also purchase various non-essential, yet desirable items such as television sets, stereo systems,

Social-Economic: Employment 71

dishwashers, etc. Most people purchase as many material goods, both necessities and luxuries, as they can afford. Directly, people work for financial reward. Indirectly and more importantly, people work to satisfy their needs of subsistence. Basically, people work to secure an income so they can achieve and maintain an adequate standard of living.

Most of the today's societies have similar employment structures and in most social systems people are employed in the same occupational roles. Let's look at the overall employment structure of the world and try to determine why it developed the way it did.

Not surprisingly, today's employment structure is based on and reflective of the cultural evolution of man. It developed the way it did because, throughout the world, people have always had to sustain themselves. All people need to eat so they raise crops and breed cattle in order to secure food for themselves. Similarly, the employment structure developed as it did because people always require protection from the elements. People need homes so they build houses, mobile trailers, and apartment buildings to live in. Likewise, in order to stay warm people chop wood, mine coal, and drill for oil to secure the resources of energy. They must also cover themselves so they shear sheep for wool, weave cotton, and produce fabrics of rayon and nylon for clothing to wear. Further, the employment structure developed the way it did because people desire a more convenient life style. They design tools, build machinery, and manufacture appliances in order to make their day-to-day living conditions easier.

An additional reason why the employment structure took the path it did has to do with advances in education. Technology expanded tremendously and in recent decades there have been significant advances in the areas of math, science, and engineering. There's been major progress within the economic spheres of agriculture, manufacturing, and energy development as well. Improvements in the health and medical fields have also occurred. In all fields of employment, people became highly skilled at their jobs. Job specialization, in fact, has become a determining factor in the technological advances of society.

In general, the structure of the labor force follows the route it's designated to follow. As new jobs are created and older ones eliminated, the makeup of society's occupational roles reflects the path that cultural development takes. With each new generation of working people, this is the case.

Looking at employment from a historical perspective, we're aware that the major social-economic systems of today developed over thousands of years. As the world's societies evolved, the employment structure changed considerably. Today, most of the world's population lives in what is known as the Industrial Age. The Industrial Age can also be referred to as the Technological Era of Man. The Technological Era is characterized with major advances in the biological, chemical, physical, and nuclear fields of science. The Technological Era is the age of electrical-mechanical science. It's an age of automation which includes the utilization of computers and intricate robotic systems. It is a period of complex machinery and heavy-duty equipment as well. Further, it's a time characterized by the introduction of modern electrical devices and household appliances. Undoubtedly, this period of development is a time of high technological specialty.

The Technological Era can be further characterized by the global distribution of goods and services. The production of manufactured goods takes place in assembly-line fashion. Everyday household appliances such as the blender, toaster, and microwave oven, as well as modern communication equipment like the telephone, computer, fax machine, radio, and television set are produced on a mass scale. It is an age of world-wide communication systems which are based on fiber optic lines, transmission towers, and space satellites. Broadcast networks utilize these technological advancements to allow for the global distribution of news and information through mass-media outlets. The Technological Era is also an age of rapid transportation systems and includes monorails, subways, high speed trains, and airplanes. It's an age characterized by highly productive agricultural consortiums as well. The consortiums are involved with the breeding and the raising of farm animals as well as with the cross-hybridization of crops and vegetables. They're involved with factory-located processing operations which include the cooking, canning, and freezing of a wide variety of food products. The Technological Era is further characterized by major advances in the areas of nutrition, health care, and medical science.

The way the major social-economic systems developed resulted in a number of improvements to the social infrastructure of the world. Among the positive changes in regard to how people live today are the following. Notable advancements have taken place in the engineering field. For example, the quality in the construction of homes and office buildings has improved greatly. So too has the structural design and construction of bridges, dams, highways, etc. Similarly, the power industry has undergone major changes as the sources of energy expanded from the fossil fuels of coal and oil to nuclear sources derived from the atom. Further, as a result of studying the phenomena of Nature, electricity was harnessed and is now used to light homes. Electricity is likewise used to power numerous types of machinery and equipment. In today's world, people are afforded a host of electrical devices like the hair dryer, can opener, and toaster. There are modern-day appliances such as the microwave oven, dishwasher, refrigerator, and freezer. Similarly, there are recently developed power tools including the weed whacker, hedge clippers, and chain saw. Also, there are more robust machinery like the lawn mower, snow blower, and garden tractor. Both the quality and quantity of manufactured products are high and their availability has helped achieve significant improvements throughout society. Further, the delivery of services designed to meet human needs has mushroomed in recent years. The broad based networks of service-orientated jobs make it much easier for people to move about and support one another. Because of the advancements made in product and process, the day-to-day living conditions of people everywhere have improved considerably.

Better education is another advantage that's representative of a specialized and more technically trained society. As we know, the level of scientific knowledge has literally skyrocketed in recent times. The benefit of an improved educational system has made equitable learning opportunities available to citizens regardless of their economic, social, or ethnic background. As would be expected, the quality of education is high in the industrialized nations of the world.

Additionally, there has been an overall improvement in the health care of people who live in modern, industrial nations. Improved nutrition, for example, has helped promote stronger and healthier individuals. Current medical treatments are characterized through better diagnosis procedures, more effective medicines, and up-to-date medical facilities which are staffed with highly trained doctors and nurses. The citizens of today are provided with better health care than were people in past societies. It goes without saying that the advances made in the fields of medical science have significantly extended the human life span.

Finally, the structure of present day social-economic systems allows for a relatively high standard of living. This results from the high level of employment that exists on a worldwide basis. Most people can find jobs and a majority of workers keep their jobs with some degree of security. Under current economic conditions, most people are able to earn job promotions and higher incomes. They do so through personal initiative and hard work. The workers become more competent and productive as they advance upwards in their particular fields of endeavor.

Although there are many advantages to present day social-economic systems, there are disadvantages as well. No system is perfect and we can cite situations in the various social-economic designs where problems arise. For example, the competitive nature, i.e., profit motivation interests of the social-economic community, may cause businesses to take short cuts in providing goods and services to consumers. Consequently, many products might be manufactured in the most cost-savings manner available. It's possible the quality of manufactured goods may be compromised as products would likely be constructed of poorer grade components. Furthermore, products may be produced under unsafe working conditions. Because of these situations, many people could be working at jobs that potentially endanger their health.

Additional health risks arise as a result of the dangerous by-products and waste products generated in the manufacturing steps. National governments set standards for safety. Nonetheless, the standards may not be strict enough or regularly enforced. Hence, there are some industries which routinely pollute the environment. The smokestacks from these industries discharge toxic particles and noxious gases into the atmosphere. Also, there are many factories which deliver chemical wastes into the drains and storm sewers. Eventually these contaminates find their way to the soil and underground water supplies.

Because of overriding economic considerations and the push for rapid production of goods, human health can be jeopardized in other ways. For example, in the effort to provide citizens with abundant food supplies the various crops, fruits, and vegetables are regularly sprayed with disease retardants including insecticides and fungicides. Likewise cattle, pigs, and chickens are subjected to various chemical additions to their food stock to promote weight gain and accelerated growth. Depending on the toxicity of these additives, such treatments can make beef, pork, and poultry hazardous for human consumption.

Irresponsibility in the areas of product manufacture and food preparation results in numerous disadvantages to the consumer. There are other examples of incongruent behavior in the business world as well. Many corporations don't always present a full report when it's time to delineate their dealings in the buying and selling of manufacturing assets and property. Often, corporations don't guarantee equity of process when it comes to the transfer of goods or the provision of services. And at times, businesses aren't forthright regarding the accuracy of advertisements on the quality of their products. Thus, hypocrisy occurs in business as well as in other areas of social life.

We should point out the shortcomings of the business world, like those described above, are due more to the way social-economic systems function rather than how they're designed. The problems arise when business and industry entities don't follow approved methods for manufacture, distribution, and sale. As in many areas of human endeavor, whenever unsafe or unfair situations arise, it's usually due to a misplacement of values.

An atmosphere of business competitiveness extends throughout the world. In such an environment, there's always the opportunity for exploitation and corruption. It spans the entire manufacturing spectrum and involves the production, distribution, and sale of goods and products. As mentioned, at times the manufacturers attempt to produce their goods in the most expedient way possible. Typically, the manufacturers attempt to be the first to the marketplace; and with the emphasis on profit, they attempt to sell their products at whatever price the traffic will bear.

In general, a government supports business enterprises through control of the nation's purse strings. A government monitors the level of its country's industrial output. It further sets the conditions for trade with other countries and establishes specific quotas and tariffs on imported goods. Thereby, the world's governments facilitate the expediency-based, profit-motivated format through which many business activities proceed.

Thus far, we've identified some beneficial and not so beneficial aspects of the world's social-economic systems in a broad sense. Now, we'll be more specific and focus on the pluses and minuses of two key social-economic systems, namely the socialistic and the free-enterprise systems.

The socialistic design is exemplified by some economic systems of Eastern Europe during the mid-to-late 1900's, as well as by the current collective-sharing architecture of communistic societies of Asia. The free enterprise design is reflected in the capitalistic framework that's been prevalent in several western nations of Europe and North America during the past couple of hundred years. The intent of both types of social-economic systems is to improve living condition and meet the day-to-day needs of people on Earth. In actual practice, both of these social-economic systems have shortcomings and leave open the opportunity for improvement.

The intent of the socialistic system is to collect the economic wealth generated in society and deliver it as uniformly as possible to the nation's citizenry. The socialistic design is based on the premise that everyone will work to support the state, and the state in turn will ensure all the members receive an equal share of benefits. However, the citizens of a socialistic nation run the risk of experiencing economic repression. They may find their system doesn't always translate into economic well-being for all the citizens when put into actual practice.

Under a socialistic system, personal incentive can be destroyed. At times, the fruits of one's labor are not returned to the individual; and too often, economic affluence tends to flow upward while the rewards of hard work don't filter down. In such an environment, economic stratification can develop and people are likely to be exploited. Although the workers are encouraged to produce and build on the premise of a humanistic agenda, they may not be rewarded fairly for their efforts. Oftentimes, the goals which individuals strive for are never or only marginally achieved.

The intent of the free enterprise design is to promote individual success relative to overall wealth generation. Indeed, several of today's social-economic systems are based upon the concept of "survival of the industrious". That is to say, the systems are designed to proceed according to the premise that people who work hard will succeed. Presumably, the people who work the hardest will succeed the most. Although this appears to be a reasonable basis for a capitalistic system, it works under some circumstances and not in others. In actual practice, some of the people are rewarded for what they do while others are not. In actual practice, far too many problems arise. Too often, within a highly complex social-economic system, power breeds more power and the people who are affluent tend to stay affluent while people who are destitute are likely to remain so. Unfortunately, a large percentage of social-economic prosperity is based upon "survival of the shrewdest" or "survival of the opportunist". In other words, there develops a stratification of people that's due to factors other than the prejudicial ones of race, sex, religion, and ethnical background. That is to say, there's economic discrimination which exists across society. Another feature typical of a capitalistic system is the tendency for intellectual discrimination to occur as well.

In a capitalistic society, a person's well-being is directly tied to one's job position and salary. Consequently, the more luxurious benefits of social life are only available to people who can afford them. In modern societies, an educational program beyond the secondary school level, i.e., college, is only available to people who can afford to pay for it. And too often, the quality of health care is available only in proportion to the amount of money people can spend on securing it. Similarly, household appliances like the dishwasher, clothes washer, clothes dryer, microwave oven, refrigerator, freezer, etc., are available only to people who have sufficiently high incomes.

If the vast majority of citizens were able to attain a more equitable standard of living then economic discrimination could be eliminated. This would happen irrespective of the type of social system people live under. However, today most of the world's population doesn't enjoy an equitably high standard of living. For a majority of social-economic systems, far too many people live in poverty. There are too many people hungry and starving. Too many people are under educated and too many are unemployed. And too many people live in unhealthy environments where there are little or no regulations regarding the quality of drinking water, the nutritional content of food, the construction of housing, or the level of safety in the workplace.

No individual who has the ability to work and perform his fair share should have to suffer such economic-based hardships. Irrespective of the social structure in place, everyone should have the opportunity to live in an economically secure environment.

A universal social-economic employment structure would incorporate key components from both the socialistic and free enterprise systems. Several of these include the following. The universal employment structure would utilize the voluntary, open-enrollment feature of the free enterprise system. Basically this means no business or industry would have to be a member of the universal employment structure unless it wanted to. Similarly, no employee or person would have to participate at a job within the universal employment structure unless he or she chose to do so. In regard to the socialistic system, the universal employment structure would utilize its common pool, all-for-one feature. For a business or industry deciding to be a member, its efforts would focus on manufacturing a product or providing a service to meet man's basic living needs such as housing, clothing, food, health care, education, etc. Likewise, an individual who chooses to participate in the universal employment structure would be guaranteed the necessities of life. One would be guaranteed the necessities, on a fair and equitable basis, provided he or she completes the required work assignments.

The social-economic malaises which occur throughout the world can be resolved and the problems of hunger, poor health, unemployment, etc.

can be addressed and solved. The wherewithal that's needed to face these challenges is available. Technologies are in place and the provisions and required materials are available. Additionally, the potential work force can be mobilized as needed. The resolution of the world's social and economic difficulties then isn't a question of resources; rather, the resolution is a question of values. More specifically, it's a question of the placement of values.

Across the world's social systems, human values must be prioritized into a hierarchy which satisfies the call for economic opportunity based on equality and justice. And how do we address this and decide where the proper placement of values ought to be? Consider the following questions on the current status of societal life and how it relates to the placement of values.

Do ill people deserve to be ill? Do hungry people deserve to be hungry, and do poor people deserve to be poor? Further, do shrewd people deserve to be better off financially than others? And do wealthy people deserve to be in control of the political and economic forces of society?

Is it more important to have most people in society healthy and well-fed, or to have only a few people well with the remaining people ill and hungry? Is it more important to have most people economically secure, or to have a few with material wealth and the rest of the population destitute?

Will the people with power be willing to give up some of their power in order to achieve a greater good? Can the well-to-do members of society help the less fortunate ones? Can people who are poor be brought to a higher living standard without having detrimental effects upon the middle and upper middle classes of society? Can compromises be reached among the various social factions so economic discrimination is eliminated?

Are humanitarian interests more important to the citizens of the world than selfishness? Are the people willing to make the required commitment; that is, secure the resources, invest the time, and do the work needed to improve society?

Importantly, can everyone who's willing to work be guaranteed the benefits he or she needs to survive? And can every individual be appropriately rewarded for his or her industriousness? In other words, can each person be adequately rewarded for his or her contributions to society?

In a population made up of diverse components, where does the balance lie in regard to the citizens achieving and sustaining an equitable standard of living? On the biological side, people show variability in their physical attributes. On the psychological side, they display differences in their mental capabilities. People have different skill sets, interests, and levels of motivation. Culturally, people vary in their ethnic backgrounds. Likewise, they vary in their political outlook and religious beliefs. Even more so, people are raised in a variety of settings and undergo different experiences in life. In light of the broad diversity to social living, what employment scenario is best suited for the majority of citizens? How should the universal social-economic system be structured so everyone's able to participate and benefit?

How will the human race go about determining the appropriate path forward and make beneficial decisions in life? If it requires a reassessment of values, will the citizens of the world reprioritize their value system to choose a proper course of action?

Let's make a definitive statement in regards to the route to success within any social-economic environment. The common denominator to all improvements achieved through social living is the endeavor of work. Indeed, every social-economic system is based upon the activity of work.

The universal social-economic system should be structured so any individual who is willing to work can work. Anyone who's able to work will have a job available to him. He or she will manufacture a product needed in society or perform a service that's useful to mankind. Each person's job accomplishments will benefit the cultural development of man. For a recompense of employment, every person will be afforded the basic necessities of life which includes allotments for living quarters, food, and clothing. Every person will be guaranteed the supplemental necessities as well. That's to say, each person will be entitled to an education and health care. Additionally, each person will be granted access to certain recreational facilities.

We might speculate where the social-economic systems of today are headed. Since man's first days on Earth, the cultural world of man has changed greatly. From it's early cave dwellers' existence to the establishment of twenty-first century industrial societies, there's been significant advancement in the arena of social living. And as extensive as cultural progress has been, the socio-economic success reflected in contemporary society is far from perfect. Indeed, the species of man has a long way to go to build an "ideal" world. As we examine the strengths and weaknesses of modern social-economic systems, we see opportunity for improvement. In today's world we know too much emphasis is placed upon material possessions. Too often, success is determined by the amount of money a person accumulates, and human worth is decided by how much power an individual wields. Such measures of social accomplishment represent a misplacement of value. At some point, the people of the world will reassess their overall value system. Someday, people will realize that humanitarian needs must take precedence over personal interests. A reassessment of the human value system is vital to the long term, socio-economic, well-being of man.

The necessities of life should be available to every person alive. Without exception, every human being is entitled to a place to live, to some kind of shelter or home. There is no reason for anyone to be denied food or clothing. Likewise, medical treatment should be available to every human being who needs it. First and foremost, life's necessities should be available to anyone who's willing to work for them. Even more so, they should be guaranteed to anyone who actually does work to earn them. This represents a basic entitlement of the people who are committed to live and work together. In addition, life's necessities should be provided to those individuals who are incapable of working because of mental or physical limitations. Such generosity represents human compassion at its highest level and is a key accomplishment of civilized social living.

In conjunction with the human desire to contribute, it is important for an individual to work in an occupation that manufactures one or more products of benefit to society. Likewise a person can better meet his purpose in life if he works in an occupation that provides a service towards the betterment of mankind.

In order to fulfill one's purpose in life, an individual must have a full-time commitment to serve others. A compassionate person then is one who donates his time and resources to help his fellow man. A compassionate person wishes to provide aid to his fellow man more than on a part-time basis. A caring human being wants to perform good deeds more than just one evening a week, or a couple of days per month. A believer in the goodness of man wants to be benevolent beyond those days he attends church. That is, as far as compassion for one's fellow man goes, a caring individual wants to assist others regardless of whether or not it's a recognized day of religious worship.

Also, a compassionate person doesn't want to do worthwhile deeds strictly through a charitable organization. He doesn't want to provide aid to his fellow man solely through work in a volunteer group which meets once or twice a month. A truly caring person doesn't want to support humanitarian causes exclusively through an organization that's supplemental to a functional, mainstream society.

Neither does a compassionate person want to provide service to his fellow man merely through proxy, say by way of a governmental agency which provides aid and welfare to needy people. A person doesn't want a governmental or religious organization to be the only means of support for those in need. The paying of taxes or providing of tithes to secure funds for destitute people isn't the preferred, long term solution to helping one's fellow man.

Instead, a sincere, caring individual wants to be associated with a "philanthropic-type" organization every day of his life. He wants to function in a social-economic system that allows him to do worthwhile deeds continuously. In other words, a human being who truly cares about his fellow man wants to participate in an employment structure that places him in an occupation, which by design, contributes to the betterment of mankind on a daily basis.

A social-economic system should be designed so the above objectives can be accomplished by any individual as he participates in his everyday work routine. A human being should be able to work in a business or industry which is dedicated to the improvement of social living. That way, the individual doesn't contribute merely once in a while. That way, one doesn't contribute only through an auxiliary, charitable-type organization. Instead, a human being is positioned to contribute every day that he's employed. A person can participate and contribute in this manner if his place of employment is geared towards advancing societal man's "quality of life".

What should the motivation be relative to determining the type of employment structure mankind ought to design? We know working at a job that brings personal satisfaction is preferred to working at a job for which one has no interest. It goes without saying that a person doesn't want to be locked into a line of work he or she detests. No individual wants to be subjected to an employment structure which is oppressive in regard to the type of physical labor or mental challenges one faces. Rather, a person wants to have some control over his own job situation. What's more, everyone wants to work in an occupation that he or she feels is important to society.

The human species has the opportunity to devise any type of socio-economic system it desires. Mankind can reengineer the entire employment world if he wishes. He can make the occupations which exist now more meaningful, responsible, and accountable. He can make the occupations significantly more respectable. Further, man can create new types of jobs across numerous and diversified fields of employment. A regenerated employment structure can design occupational roles which are as varied as the range of human interests.

Overall, the employment structure should reflect the goals of the cultural development of man. All the jobs in the employment structure should provide mankind with the opportunity to fulfill his purpose in life. A person ought to be able to choose an occupation that he feels is most rewarding, and to facilitate it, a person needs the opportunity to secure an adequate education. One must have access to the training needed to become competent in the occupation of his choosing.

We should emphasize the occupational roles of a redesigned employment structure will have a built-in plan for self-actualization. A key objective of the universal institution of employment is to allow each individual to achieve a sense of accomplishment for his or her efforts. Thereby, every person can pursue an occupation with the knowledge that a basic design of the employment structure is to improve "quality of human life" throughout the world.

The ultimate goal of a redesigned employment structure then is twofold. It is to provide a person with the necessary resources, including the education and skill set, to secure work in an occupation in which he's interested. Additionally, it's to ensure the occupation a person pursues is one which supports the quest to achieve man's purpose in life. Such an occupation can exist for everyone. And should the occupation not be in place, the species of man has the ability to create it.

How would a realignment of the world's employment structure come about? To begin with, mankind has to assess the current occupational roles of society. Then he must redesign those roles if necessary. With that being done, he must establish new roles wherever needed. And for the most part, mankind ought to establish roles that reflect the social-economic system we've described.

A universal social-economic system would install an employment structure that provides an equitable means to earn a living in order to meet one's needs of survival. First of all, the universal social-economic system would ensure that everyone in society has an adequate place to live. Housing centers will be built and maintained to make sure people are protected from inclement weather conditions including excessive hot and cold temperatures, as well as the atmospheric turbulences of rain, snow, wind, etc. The housing centers will consist of apartments, condominiums, single-family homes, and multiple-family dwellings. The social-economic system would establish codes for the construction and maintenance of all residential and business structures including houses, apartment complexes, retail outlets, office buildings, and manufacturing plants.

Second, this system would guarantee that all people in society have adequate clothing. The institution would index and monitor the quality of wearing apparel. Clothing standards on types of material, durability, and workmanship will be established. Factories will be built to satisfy the clothing requirements of society. Also, there will be factories built to manufacture footwear including slippers, shoes, sneakers, galoshes, and boots. There will be factories constructed to produce outerwear apparel such as overcoats, parkas, raincoats, hats, gloves, etc.

Third, the universal social-economic system would ensure that food is available to everyone. The institution would require that standards be set on the quality and nutritional value of food. There will be agricultural centers established to provide adequate food supplies. There will be areas of land set aside to grow food crops like wheat, oats, and corn; areas set aside for food plants such as asparagus, broccoli, and rhubarb; and regions set aside for vegetables including potatoes, beans, lettuce, carrots, onions, etc. There will be fruit-tree farms in operation for harvest of fruits such as the apple, pear, peach, plum, orange, pineapple, etc. Livestock centers will be established to provide the meat supplies of beef, mutton, pork, and venison. There will be farms to raise poultry, including Cornish hens, chickens, turkeys, pheasants, ducks, etc. Fish hatcheries will be operated to supply fresh water foods like trout, bass, pike, and salmon. Fish farms will provide other seafood products such as lobster, shrimp, and crab. Furthermore, food-processing plants will be constructed and made operational to process all food products whether fruit, vegetable, fish, poultry, or meat. The food will be cooked and subsequently canned or frozen. The food supplies will then be distributed across the land to meet the subsistent and nutrimental needs of society.

Thus, the items and products associated with the human needs of food, clothing, and shelter will be available to all people who work in, or are supported by, the universal social-economic system.

A redirected social-economic system would provide the necessities of life and essential services to those people who work to earn them. The main difference between a redirected universal social-economic system and the current ones is the following. Under a newly designed employment structure there would be supplemental necessities of life guaranteed to all citizens. The supplemental necessities would include education, health care, and recreation. In addition, there would be amenities in the fields of communication and transportation. The supplemental necessities and amenities are present above and beyond the essentials of food, clothing, and shelter. Their availability is assured and therefore not dependent upon basic welfare services as provided under the current social-economic systems via government agencies, church groups, and charitable organizations. Hence, under a redirected social-economic system the necessities of life, both basic and supplemental, would be available to everyone. People wouldn't have to seek them out nor depend upon charitable organizations to secure them.

There's but one criterion required in having the necessities of life available to everyone in society. That criterion is: the necessities will only be provided to the people who work to earn them. Except for individuals who are mentally or physically incapable of being employed, everyone must work within the universal institution of employment to be guaranteed the necessities of life.

What about the people in society who out-and-out refuse to work? Those individuals, who refuse to work even though they're capable, would have to rely upon family members, the church, and charitable organizations within the private sector to sustain their needs. Hopefully, they would come to realize that anything of value in life comes by way of faith and commitment; or in other words, the willingness to put forth the effort.

It's important to note the structure of a universal employment institution relieves everyone from the responsibility of looking for ways to meet his or her purpose in life. The system would be designed so an individual's purpose is satisfied automatically by way of one's occupation. As discussed, the universal employment institution will meet all of man's personal survival needs. It will also satisfy man's educational and medical needs, as well as his requirements for recreation. Further, the universal employment institution would lay the foundation for man to focus on improving the welfare of other creatures of life. That is, it would provide mankind with the mechanism to enhance the earth's environment and its several ecosystems.

It's of interest to note how important the activity of work is to the biological and psychological well-being of man. Work is an essential requirement or charge to the positive side of human nature. To work is to help keep the human body healthy and in good physical condition. Psychologically, to work promotes self-esteem. It builds an internal awareness of self-worth for any individual who makes a useful product or provides a needed service. In such spirit, a human being improves society through the activity of gainful employment.

A redirected social-economic system would provide the means for every person to earn a living. It would establish a secure employment network, well-founded in structure as well as operation, to advance social life. As described, under a revised universal social-economic system, every person will be required to work and the employment structure would be designed so everyone would have the opportunity to work at an occupation that suits his interests. Further, everyone would be able to work in an occupation that makes a contribution to society.

A person would enter one's respective profession and do the best he could because he wanted to. It doesn't matter if the occupation is that of a doctor, lawyer, or schoolteacher. It doesn't matter if the occupation is a cab driver, auto mechanic, or factory worker. It doesn't matter if the occupation is a shoe salesman, airline passenger screener, or pizza deliveryman. A person would not enter a profession for the reason of acquiring prestige, power, or financial reward. Rather, he would enter an occupation to support his fellow man and provide a service of humanitarian worth.

A major undertaking of a redirected employment structure would be to upgrade the vast majority of jobs within the current social-economic systems. Although all occupations will be affected, this process would particularly benefit the people who are employed in the more menial jobs. Whether in the fields of food service, nursing, or janitorial care, all of the jobs would be upgraded. Whether in the areas of shipping or mail delivery, all jobs will be made more accountable. And whether in the fields of maintenance or sanitation, all jobs will be made more challenging. Whether in the arenas of manufacturing or farming, all jobs will be made more meaningful. And whether in construction or the trades, all jobs will be made more fulfilling.

Job positions will be redefined. Wherever possible, the jobs in all fields of employment will be made more technically challenging. Thus enhanced from a technical perspective, the jobs would require a greater skill set to complete. This would naturally involve a higher level of training and thereby result in a better skilled workforce.

Current job duties would be expanded so greater decision-making power is delegated to the employees. The transfer of decision-making from the managerial to worker's positions will likely lead to occupational roles characterized with more intellectual challenges. And in order to satisfy these challenges, more input of thoughts and ideas will be required from employees as they go about meeting their daily work assignments.

The main emphasis of the upgrades would be to restructure jobs so they hold greater responsibility. Since workers will be expected to take on more responsibility, the occupational roles must be designed to have an appropriate level of accountability as well. Hence, the upgraded job positions would exact an acceptable level of expectation and commitment from all workers.

The newly designed job positions would also require more flexibility from the employees as there will be more cross-training on related jobs within one's field of employment. Thereby, the workers should be more adaptable. Accompanying the improved training and greater flexibility will be a more equitable distribution of labor across the workforce. The result of a revamped employment structure then will be a more balanced alignment of job positions.

Finally, all job positions must be satisfying to the people who work. The occupational roles will be designed so all job positions are inherently beneficial to society. Not only will the design of the jobs be contributive, but the positions will be structured so they're recognized as such by everyone in society.

A significant benefit of a redesigned employment structure would result in the employees being respected for their contributions to society. The prestige of all jobs will be enhanced. The prestige factor would arise from either the product manufactured or the service provided by the employee. It wouldn't arise from a job's particular ranking in a hierarchy of supervisory or managerial positions.

How might a new social-economic system be structured? The new social-economic system would contain its constituent businesses and industries. All of the businesses and industries will be designed to provide the materials, goods, and services that meet the basic and supplemental needs of man. All the businesses and industries will be dedicated to the improvement of social living. The industries will be in the area of energy production and include the coal, oil, natural gas, and electric companies. Energy production venues also include the power plants that derive energy from solar, wind, hydroelectric, and nuclear sources. The industries will be in the area of transportation. These consist of freight and passenger carriers as well as the trucking firms, shipping companies, railroad systems, and airline networks. The businesses will be in the area of communications.

These include the telegraph and telephone companies. They take in the radio and television stations as well. The industries will also be in the area of housing and construction. Such industries include the lumber companies and steel mills. They involve the cement and concrete firms. They include the furniture manufacturers as well. Further, the businesses and industries will be in the area of wearing apparel. These businesses include the clothing manufactures and producers of footwear.

A new social-economic system will contain its own agricultural centers. The agricultural centers will be responsible for the production and distribution of food. They include the fruit orchards. They include farmlands set aside to raise crops and vegetables. They also include the dairy farms. They include the poultry farms as well as sheep and cattle ranches. They include businesses that process food, including the canning companies, meat packing firms, and frozen food companies. They further include businesses that transport and deliver food and food products to all the citizenry.

All the jobs in business and industry within the universal social-economic system will benefit society. The social-economic system will be structured so the businesses and industries willing to participate are able to do so. By voluntary agreement, businesses or industries from the private sector may join the newly formed universal social-economic system. They would not, however, compete with similar businesses and industries within the private sector. The businesses and industries in the non-public sector will continue to function as independently owned-and-operated entities. Nonetheless, like all major enterprises that comprise the several institutions of society, they will be subject to the national laws established by government.

From an operational standpoint, each major institution of society will function separately from the others. Each institution will have its own rules and regulations. Each will have its own governing body. The employment institution, for instance, would stand independent of the institution of government. It would neither be administered by, nor financially dependent upon, government. Consistent with its role regarding all other institutions, the institution of government would guarantee the institution of employment's right to exist. Government will be the only institution with an arresting (police) force, a judgment (court) force, and a punishment (penal) force. Government would ensure the businesses and industries within the employment structure interact justly with one another and treat their employees with fairness and equality. It would ensure that business and industries provide safe work conditions as well as equitable pay. It would ensure that businesses and industries manufacture products which meet quality, reliability, and safety standards.

The universal institution of employment will function independent of the other institutions of society as well. It won't be an agency of another institution. Neither will it be directed or financed by another institution. Nevertheless, the employment institution will have close ties to the other institutions. Like the institution of religion, its founding premise is based on a commitment to the betterment of mankind. And like the institution of government, its operational design is geared toward justice and equality.

By definition, the universal institution of employment will be a publicly-based system. The employment world of man will continue to consist of privately-owned businesses and industries, as well as the public enterprises. As indicated, the public components will automatically be full-time members of the universal employment structure. However, the businesses and industries from the private sector will be members to the extent they want to be. The private business and industries can voluntarily join and contribute at the level they deem appropriate.

It should be pointed out that citizens who chose to remain exclusively within the private sector need not participate in the universal social-economic system as described. The individuals, who work entirely at private sector jobs to meet all their needs of subsistence, health care, education, etc., can do so and remain independent of the universally-based institutions of society.

From a structural design, there will be several key divisions to the universal employment institution. One will be dedicated to housing and it would involve the coordination of all participant enterprises that provide housing and housing allotments. A second division will be responsible for the coordination of all food allotments. It'll coordinate the entire disposition of food products from food production, to processing, to distribution. A third division will be responsible for coordination of the production and dissemination of all clothing allotments. Additional divisions will be responsible for their respective areas of societal life, i.e., education, health care, communication, transportation, etc. Each major division will consist of occupations dedicated to that particular field of endeavor. Each will contain jobs in the manufacturing and service-orientated realms. Each will contain management and employee positions. These divisions will interface with the managerial boards of their respective universal institutions of society, which are described in the following chapters.

From an operational design the universal employment institution will have its own managerial network. It will consist of a management hierarchy that's headed by a governing board that's made up of representatives chosen from the various occupational divisions referred to in the previous paragraph. Each division will provide governing board candidates who are selected from their respective participating businesses and industries. The governing board will contain both employers and employees who would serve for predetermined lengths of time. The representatives to the governing board shall be selected through a fair and open elective process.

The goods and services to be guaranteed to the people who participate in the redesigned social-economic system shall be determined by the governing board. The governing board will determine both the quality standards of the goods manufactured and the performance standards of the services provided. In regard to produced goods, it shall determine the variety, frequency, and amount of merchandise the citizens receive. It will likewise determine other material-based benefits including monetary allotments for housing, food, clothing, medicine, etc. In regard to services performed, the governing board shall determine the nature and extent of duties that people are expected to deliver. It will likewise decide service-based amenities which are available in the areas of education, communication, transportation, recreation, etc.

The governing board shall determine the breakdown of job responsibilities throughout the institution of employment. It shall determine the criteria for the amount and nature of work to be completed in all occupations. It shall determine the employee's input that's required for the employee to receive the benefits of subsistence support, education, and health care. As mentioned, it will set the range of entitlements of food, clothing, shelter, etc., the employee can receive.

Across the employment spectrum the governing board shall establish criteria relating to monetary compensation. That is, it will determine job classification levels and set pay grades pertinent to those levels. It will determine wages and salaries, working hours, overtime and vacation pay, etc. It will determine sick pay, compensation for injury on the job, and time off allotments for disability. It will also determine the compensation for military reserve duty, jury duty, maturity leave, and so forth.

The governing board shall establish the mechanism for job advancements and promotions, as well as the conditions for job transfers within the workplace. Also, the governing board will institute a jurisprudence process to resolve employee complaints and job-related grievances. Finally, it shall set the safety standards which must be in place for each type of job.

We note the governing board will work closely with the universal institution of government to ensure the employment institution's operating principles are in agreement with the workplace product and process regulations drawn up and enforced by the legislative and executive branches of government.

How will the universal institution of employment function in regard to an individual's participation? One employment design would permit an individual to hold two jobs. The first job would be at a business or industry within the private sector. The second job would be in the newly formed universal employment institution. Through employment in the restructured social-economic system, a person will earn the necessities of life for himself and his family such as food, clothing, and health care. He will acquire a standard housing unit to live in, or earn a housing allotment to put towards a dwelling of his choice. Additionally, he will receive a free education as well as access to public recreational facilities. The job in the private sector will allow the individual to earn money in order to acquire other necessities and luxuries as desired. He could use the compensation from the private sector job to enhance his standard of living, such as making an upgrade to his housing, etc.

Another employment design would have the individual working at only one job, either inside or outside of the universal institution of employment. If a person's place of employment was either in the public or private realm only, then he would have to work at that job for a sufficient portion of his lifetime to secure all benefits, material or otherwise, that he needs to support his family. This is similar to many of today's employment systems whereby an employee is gainfully employed a specified number of hours per week, typically forty, and works at that job until he reached retirement age.

There are several options available as to how a person is able to achieve the key benefits afforded through the universal employment institution. One option allows a person to earn credit towards the acquisition of the necessities of life by working for a prescribed length of time. A person might work a minimum number of hours per week, perhaps sixteen to twenty-four hours. Or, he might work a minimum number of days per week, say two to three days. Or, he might work a minimum number of years of his career, perhaps sixteen to twenty-four years. By working at a job within the employment institution for a specified period of time, the individual would be guaranteed the necessities of life. He would be guaranteed the basic necessities for himself and his family throughout their lifetime.

As indicated, an employee could work in both systems if he desired. The person could participate in a private sector business and a public sector enterprise at the same time. That is, he could work at both jobs across a specified time frame of perhaps a year, two year, five year, or longer period. The person could split his or her work assignments on both jobs at ratios say of 10:90, 20:80, 25:75, 30:70, 40:60, or 50:50. Alternatively, the person could participate in the private and public sector jobs at separate times; that is, at different stages during his or her working career.

During the minimum period of service in the universal employment institution, the fruits of one's labor would go to improve overall quality of societal life. That is to say, a person would work to provide the basic necessities of food, clothing, and housing for his family specifically, and for those who were incapable of supporting themselves in general. He would also work to improve comprehensive health care as well as expand the overall quality of public education. Through his efforts in the employment world, every individual will provide a valuable service to all members of society. Ultimately, one's efforts will help promote and protect the lives of all living creatures. That's because every person's accomplishments will help man in his quest to take on the responsibility of gardening and governing Nature.

If a person wants additional benefits including certain non-essential goods, items, etc., he would have to work beyond the minimal period of service. If a person wants additional money for recreational or entertainment purposes, he would have to work extra. The extra period of time a person works depends upon personal initiative and the cost of what one wants to obtain. If a person's only job is with the universal institution of employment then he would have to work extra hours at that job to secure the additional benefits. Optionally, he could work extra hours at another job that's associated with his line of work within the universal employment institution. If a person holds two separate jobs, one in the universal employment institution and one in the private sector, then the job with the universal employment institution will support his basic living needs. The other job, the one in the private sector, will support the additional benefits or amenities he wishes to obtain.

A person who works in the universal employment institution can attain extra housing credits if he wants to purchase a more expensive home. He can earn additional credits if he wants to purchase a vacation home, a yacht, etc. A person can also earn credits in order to gain enhanced benefits in the areas of food allotment, clothing, education, medical care, recreation, and so forth. A person will earn supplemental credits by working on his job for an extended period of time, beyond the standard required period.

The types of businesses and industries belonging in the employment institution are those dedicated to meeting the fundamental needs of mankind. They are businesses and industries which produce goods that satisfy the basic requirements for shelter, clothing, and food. The additional requirements of life such as education, health care, and recreation are also of consequence. The businesses and industries that function to satisfy these needs are also important to a restructured social-economic system. Thus, the mission of all enterprises participating in the universal employment institution is to advance the accomplishments of social life on an all-encompassing scale.

As far as the employment institution's support of education is concerned, a person's formal training would be paid by working for a specified period of time. The educational allotment will cover the costs of nursery school, elementary school, secondary school, and college. The employment requirement to gain the lifetime educational benefits would likely require working two or more years in a sanctioned occupation. A sanctioned occupation would be identified as one that either generates a product or provides a service which meets one of man's basic needs. Such an occupation may or may not be part of the universal employment institution. In fact, the occupations could reside in any of the major institutions of society.

The occupations might reside in the institution of government where the assignments could involve those of the postal service or military. They could also include positions involved with fire fighting or police work. The occupations might reside in the institution of ecology. In ecology, they could involve jobs in forestry, landscaping, park maintenance, or wildlife refuge service. They could also include agricultural assignments such as those associated with animal husbandry or veterinary medicine. The occupations might belong to the institution of transportation and involve assignments in baggage handling or ticket taking. The occupations could belong to the institution of communication and involve jobs relating to internet access, cellular phone operation, or satellite dish installation.

Further, the occupations could be associated with the institution of health care and include positions with an ambulance service. Likewise, they could involve assignments in a medical research laboratory or a nursing home for senior citizens.

The education-occupational connection would entail a cooperative arrangement set up between the place of employment and the institution of education. A person will be entitled to a high quality education whether it involves attaining a secondary school diploma, becoming certified as a craftsman in a trade, or earning a doctoral degree from a college or university.

There would be a similar arrangement for health care coverage. Through credit earned in the employment world, a person will be entitled to free health care throughout his lifetime. This will involve allotments for medicines and therapeutic drugs. It will involve allotments for physical and mental exams. It will also involve allotments for diagnostic testing, hospitalization, and surgery. It will cover all visits to dentists, doctors, surgeons, psychoanalysts, and psychologists. It will cover all treatments by chiropractors and physical therapists as well. The expenses incurred from consultations and treatments performed by all health care providers would thereby be covered. Every person who participates in the universal health care program would work for a specified period of time; that is, time long enough to attain all the designated quality-of-life credits.

At this point, it's worthwhile to clarify what we mean when we talk about the public and private sectors of society. When we discuss the public sector, we are referring to elements of the universal institutions that involve society at large, particularly those that deal with the socio-economic status of a nation. These are the primary institutions of employment, education, health care, and recreation as well as the requisite institutions of communication, transportation, energy, environment, utility-services, discovery, etc. Obviously, the key institution in this mix is the institution of employment. It's the one that provides the majority of jobs dedicated to providing the products and services that are required to keep a social system functioning.

The public-based components are the industries, companies, commercial businesses, retailers, utilities, and service organizations that are owned and operated by the institution itself. Likewise, the components are entities sponsored by elements within the institutions; that is, sponsors such as government agencies, religious organizations, educational institutes, and so forth. The public-based components also include the enterprises, such as corporations, which are owned and operated by shareholders who have invested in the enterprises through the purchase of stocks and bonds, etc.

The private sector, on the other hand, would include businesses, industries, utilities, retail outlets, etc., that are owned and operated by self-employed and self-managed individuals, groups, or associations. These enterprises are self-supporting and manufacture a product or provide a service with the intent of earning an income. Income from their endeavors will go to purchase raw materials and supplies, pay utilities and overhead costs, fund a work force, pay taxes, and earn a profit. A portion of the profit would be used to enhance the future growth of the enterprises.

How will the universal institution of employment function in regard to the private sector's involvement? Although the employment institution would predominately consist of publicly-based businesses and industries, it would likely contain a substantial number of privately owned enterprises. The percentage of private-owned businesses might vary significantly from one area of employment to another. In some areas of employment, say food processing, the percentage of privately owned business may be high; whereas in other areas, say clothing manufacturing, it could be quite low.

The universal institution of employment would offer the option for a business or industry to participate on a part-time basis. That's to say, the business entity could function independently within the private sector of society yet also serve to the extent it wanted to in the public sector, which is the universal employment institution. It could split its raw materials, commitment of time, human resources, and manufacturing output between the private and public sectors. The level of commitment an enterprise devotes to the two sectors could vary, say at ratios of 10:90, 20:80, 25:75, 30:70, 40:60, or 50:50. The private enterprises are free to move into and out of the universal employment institution as they wish. If desired, they could change their participation status on a year-by-year basis.

We should note that the participating businesses and industries, privately or publicly-based, would provide the resources and raw materials needed to generate the products for manufacture. Once the raw materials were processed and converted into useable products, they would be delivered via voucher, credit, or actual merchandise to participants within the employment structure. Additionally, the goods and products would be available for sale to the general citizenry. In a similar vein, participating members of the universal social-economic system would ensure the services they provide are made available to society at large.

Regardless of its structure or governing hierarchy, there's a need for a universal social-economic system. Compared to current economic systems, a universal social-economic system would better meet the day-to-day needs of mankind.

A new universal social-economic system will provide jobs for people who want an alternate place of employment. It'll provide jobs in the public sector rather than the private sector. The universal social-economic system will provide the opportunity to obtain work for everyone who needs a job, as well as provide a place of employment for everyone who wishes to contribute to the advancement of societal life.

The minimum amount of work a person must perform to be eligible for the basic necessities has to do with several factors. For one, it depends upon the level of necessities and amenities the person wishes to receive. The more benefits one desires relative to subsistence, education, medical care, etc., the longer an individual will have to work. Likewise, the greater the value of specific amenities desired, the longer the person will have to remain within the universal institution of employment. Additional factors have to do with the stage of one's life, or more specifically, the type of work he or she is performing. For the participants in their late teens and early twenties, the type of work performed as well as their degree of contributions will be fairly equivalent, for it's likely they are going to school and working part-time, or working in supportive positions such as assistants, technicians, apprentices, etc., to more key occupations. Generally, they work at jobs supporting the drive engines of society, which are the jobs that produce the goods and provide the services important to the major institutions of society.

Other factors have to do with the level of various employment positions relative to the overall needs of society. All occupations would be pro-rated relative to the combination of time and productivity goals that are required for the participants to receive the same level of benefits and amenities. Either time-wise or based upon the importance of the products and services performed, there would be a scale established whereby occupational roles are rated regarding their comparative value to society. For adults who work a significant portion of their life in the universal employment structure, the role of a doctor or dentist may require less involvement of time, but nonetheless an equivalent level of accomplishment, as compared to the role of a bus driver or auto mechanic. In other words, the contributions and rewards will be tied to the overall performance requirements of pre-determined and pre-defined occupations.

A universal social-economic system would provide equal opportunity for employment regardless of a person's training or formal education, regardless of one's physical strength or level of intelligence, and regardless of one's race or ethnic background. It would provide equal employment opportunity regardless of a person's religious beliefs, political convictions, economic wealth, or social status. Further, it would provide equal opportunity of employment regardless of one's age or sex. Teenage children, young adults, adults, and senior citizens, whether male or female, will all have a role in this universal social-economic system.

As we said, the universal social-economic system won't exclude people because of age. Every person from one to one hundred years old will have an opportunity to benefit from this social-economic design. All individuals will be able to contribute to the system during their employable period of life, say from sixteen to seventy years of age. During that time they will have the opportunity to devote a portion of their working career to the universal employment structure. In doing so, they'll be able to earn a lifetime of amenities to sustain their well-being.

The design of the social-economic system is aimed at satisfying man's innate desire to help those in need. Everyone should be afforded the opportunity for medical care, an education, and non-poverty living conditions. Although the opportunities for these benefits should be guaranteed to all, there are circumstances which can't be controlled in regard to who's actually able to earn the benefits. For sure, there are some people who may be ill their whole life.

There are individuals who are physically or mentally unable to work. For example, there are people who have a terminal illness like cancer. They have to deal with their illness and worry about it every day. They may be in pain. They may not feel well and might suffer from the side effects of chemotherapy or radiation treatments. They may be nervous, depressed, and unable to sleep at night. They may have little energy and be limited in their physical capabilities as well. Thus, our challenge is to help those people live the highest quality life that's possible for them.

Additionally, there are individuals who must be supported until they're able to work to support themselves. For example, there are people in the world who have no or little education. There are people who live in poverty. Until these people are afforded a meaningful education and are able to raise themselves out of poverty by way of gainful employment, they need assistance. Also, there are people who experience accidents and suffer major disabilities or even paralysis. Likewise, there are people who are victims of violent crimes such as rape, beatings, etc., and need time to recover. Further, there are people who suffer the hardships of natural disasters, such as floods, forest fires, tornados, etc. Whatever their misfortunes, it's our responsibility to help all of these people reach a position whereby they can live under the best conditions possible.

A universal social-economic system would provide the material, technical, and financial support needed to advance societal life. By its very design, the employment institution would function to take care of the poor, needy, and destitute until they can take care of themselves. By its very design, it would provide continual support to the handicapped, ill, and infirmed. By working at their jobs in the universal employment institution, all employed individuals would contribute to this cause.

If they so wished, people could provide additional support to their fellow man by volunteering to serve in a social service organization, or by making a financial contribution to a local charity. Nevertheless, to satisfy society's humanitarian needs, people wouldn't have to perform volunteer work. Nor would they have to make a charitable contribution. Rather by going to work every day and performing their job duties, they will accomplish this goal. The employees will be meeting their humanitarian obligations based on the design of the universal institution of employment.

If we look at the various age groups across society, we see the preschoolers and school-age children will be engaged in the educational aspects of a universal social-economic system. The teenagers and young adults will be involved in both the educational and employment aspects. The adults and senior citizens will certainly participate in the employment sector. They might be involved in the educational phase as well.

The universal employment institution then isn't designed for just the people of working age, those between sixteen and seventy years old. Rather it is designed for everyone. Without exception, everyone's livelihood is dependent upon the employment structure. A universal employment institution would ensure there's opportunity for any person to contribute to society through gainful employment. Any person will contribute to society as long as he's physically and mentally capable of doing so.

A restructured social-economic system would be particularly supportive of the elderly people. To appreciate this, consider the situation of the elderly and their expected role in society. We know that a person can retire from his place of employment at the age of sixty-five or more. However, that person does not retire from his or her involvement in social-economic affairs. He or she still has an important role to play in service to one's fellow man.

To take advantage of the potential contributions of senior citizens, general attitudes about employment opportunities for the elderly must be broadened. Social attitudes in regard to maintaining a mandatory retirement age need to be reevaluated. Older people should continue to be employed provided they are physically and mentally sound and still want to be employed. The senior citizens ought to continue to function at meaningful jobs, at least at meaningful jobs within the universal employment structure.

Senior citizens should be permitted to continue to work in occupational roles that contribute to the advancement of society. There appears to be little need for modern science to prolong the human life span merely for the sake of extending it. For what advantage is there of dying at one hundred, instead of eighty-five, if there's nothing constructive to do with one's life in old age? What advantage is there for living a longer life, if at eighty-five a person feels he's become a burden to society? A human being's value to the social-economic world knows no "artificial" parameters such as age. To live an extended and satisfying life span, a person must continue to have a sense of worth. It's the sense of worth that makes his or her potential contributions not only useful, but desirable.

Elderly people can work at part-time jobs say for two or three hours a day in business and industry. Indeed, they can work two or three days a week at jobs in the universal social-economic system. The elderly can work part-time at jobs in museums, libraries, and schools. They can work in day care centers, hospitals, and nursing homes. They can work at jobs in government agencies such as the post office, police department, bureau of motor vehicles, or department of social services. The elderly can work on conservation projects in parks or at recreational facilities, etc.

At this point, let's discuss the rationale for a need to realign the institution of employment. What's the justification for restructuring this major institution of society? What obligation does man have to provide widespread benefits to his fellow citizen, and what's the precedence to provide broad human services via the employment structure?

The obvious response to these questions is the following. All of the recommendations that we propose are being done anyhow! Society already does provide significant welfare benefits to people. Society does provide broad human services in one form or another. People do live in homes and they are buying food and clothing for themselves. People do get medical attention and they educate their children. Further, people do work in business and industry to manufacture an assortment of goods and products, and they do provide numerous services for one another on a daily basis.

Under current employment structures, society's financial wherewithal is determined by the stability of economic conditions. As such, many of today's social-economic systems are structured in ways that promote the accruement of debt on both an individual and corporate scale. This, in turn, has a deciding effect on how successful the social-economic programs end up. One of the key aspects of a redesigned employment structure is based on the premise that no debt will be generated. Progress would depend upon the level of financial and material resources that are available to administer the employment program. It would proceed at a pace determined by the availability of materials, supplies, and so forth. It would proceed at a pace based on the size of the workforce and the number of businesses and industries that participate.

A problem with several current social systems is the fact they provide economic benefits to people with varying degrees of success. A restructured social-economic system is necessary because it would ensure there's a more equitable distribution of goods and services to all the citizens. The distribution would be based on a required level of work that's completed by each and every person who is able to work. Furthermore, there wouldn't be an accumulation of personal or national debt since the scope of the program depends upon the degree of available resources, i.e., manpower, materials, supplies, etc.

Let's now take a look at the employment structure from a practical standpoint. Let's review some realities of life and identify events that we know are certain to occur in one's lifetime. Consider the following. A person is born. He needs food to remain alive and grow. He needs clothes. He also needs a home. A person needs to be educated and he requires health care. In addition, a person needs to participate in recreational activities. Finally, and of high importance is the fact that a person must work. He must be employed at a task in one capacity or another. That is, a person must occupy his time in a constructive and worthwhile endeavor.

The basic requirements for human survival are well known. In order for mankind to meet its needs, some type of organized social-economic system must function in society. As a matter of fact, some type of social-economic system has always operated. At this point in history, man is in a unique position. The recent technological advances have freed a majority of people from the requirement of working fifteen to sixteen hours a day just to survive. The world contains a sufficiently high number of people who can split up the requirements for meeting the survival needs of mankind. One segment of the population can produce the food that's required; another segment can produce the wearing apparel; and a third segment can build the homes that are needed. And so it goes, with other segments of people "free" to pursue other important goals. Thus, each segment or group of people generates its own contribution to society, and each has sufficient time and energy to pursue additional worthwhile objectives. The net result is the human species has time to devote itself to activities other than those crucial for biological survival. Hence, mankind has both the time and capability to design the type of employment structure he wishes. If desired, he can reshape the world's current social-economic systems. And without a shortage of resources, man has the means to build and manage a newly designed, universal social-economic system.

To work to remain alive is to work to uphold the first and fundamental purpose of mankind. That purpose is to satisfy man's biological or composed needs of respiration, digestion, assimilation, circulation, etc. Notwithstanding, the secondary purpose must be upheld as well. As we know, the secondary purpose is to live as a human being is supposed to live. On a global scale, man's secondary purpose can best be achieved through participation in a social-economic system that affords the opportunity to improve the overall quality of life. That means it's the opportunity to work in a social-economic system which is geared towards the satisfaction of man's psychological drives, needs, and goals.

As we know, all institutions of society such as government, religion, health care, and education, are important. However, the employment institution is distinguishably important. The employment institution serves as the catalyst for social living. That is, it bridges the gap across the several institutions of mankind and stands as a sustaining force that allows a person to live a secure life. It's a sustaining force because every occupation in the institution of employment can provide the opportunity to improve the state of social living. Further, every occupation within the employment institution can be directed towards helping man pursue his purpose in life.

Without question, the institution of employment is crucial to the well-being of mankind. On a broader level, the employment structure provides for the production and distribution of goods and services that are necessary to society. It allows for materials and products to be manufactured which couldn't adequately be generated by individuals working alone. Similarly, it allows for the widespread performance of services in areas of transportation, communication, and so forth. Additionally, it improves the quality of life due to its contributions to the field of education. Indeed, the employment structure helps society progress through its involvement in research and development, including its sponsorship of studies in medicine and health care.

On a more personal level, the employment institution is vital for it offers a human being the means to earn a living. It provides the avenue for a person to meet his needs and thereby survive in the world. As stated early on, a human being is an active and functioning creature. In order to attain one's purpose in life, a human being must work. Indeed, the drive to work is fundamental to human nature and an individual must continue to plan, build, and produce. Thus, to experience a satisfying life, a person must be employed in some type of occupational role. A universal employment structure will provide the opportunity to work in an occupation that helps man meet his purpose in life.

7

Health, Education, Recreation

In chapter 6, we've discussed the basic entitlements of food, clothing, and shelter, which are guaranteed to people who work in the universal institution of employment. Closely connected to life's necessities are the supplemental requirements of health care, education, and recreation. For sure, health care is a necessity of life and no less valuable than food, clothing, or shelter. Education likewise is important and necessary. Education promotes intellectual and emotional growth and helps an individual realize his potential in life. As we know, one's success in the business world depends to a large extent upon the formal schooling and training he receives. Finally, the realm of recreation is certainly a significant component of human life. Recreation provides a person with the avenue to relaxation and enjoyment. Without question, recreation is vital to both the physical and psychological well-being of man.

Of paramount concern to every person is the state of his or her health. This covers one's physical and mental well-being. A person's physical health and state of mind are inseparable. The brain is connected via the nervous system to every sector of the body, and if a physical problem arises somewhere in the body, a stimulus from the affected region is sent to the brain. The intensity of the stimulus determines the seriousness of the mind's interpretation of the discomfort. When a problem arises, the physical discomfort can affect the person's mental well-being on either a short or long term basis. In a similar fashion, the experience of emotional disharmony can influence the state of one's physical health. That is, a mental disturbance can at times bring about a physical ailment of the body. As with the case of an emotional problem brought on by a physical ailment, the extent of the physical discomfort caused by an emotional disturbance can be immediate or long lasting. In ways we've described here, a person's emotional "happiness" and physical well-being are definitely dependent upon one another.

As we know, every person desires good physical health. No one wants to be ill and experience a cold, a fever, or the flu. Likewise, no one wants to suffer from a disease. No person wants to experience weakness of muscle, physical pain, or undergo a broken bone. Similarly, everyone wants to be free from emotional harm. No one wants to be subjected to anxiety, fear, or live in a state of depression. What every person desires is good health. Every person wants to feel good physically, and everyone wishes to maintain a positive attitude in day-to-day living.

At this point, it might be worthwhile to discuss man's perception of good health. What's the definition of good health and what should our goals toward good health be? In many respects a person's concept of good health is similar to one's interpretation of everyday life. That is, once a person has good health it's not thought of as an advantage in and of itself. It's not necessarily considered to be a plus. And like our overall perception of life, good health is taken for granted. Nevertheless, when a person's health is put in jeopardy, he becomes very concerned. When a person experiences poor health, good health becomes an objective of high priority and a goal to pursue.

Throughout history, people have always tried to maintain a state of good health. People have always sought medical attention when stricken with illness or disease. Whether an individual seeks out a witch doctor or a medicine man, he's in search of a treatment for his ailment. And whether one seeks out a general practitioner or a surgeon, he's in pursuit of expertise in the area of health care. Everyone pursues the medical treatment that he thinks is appropriate to remain healthy.

Good health then is a goal pursued by everyone. It's the goal of the universal institution of health care as well. As a goal, good health can be defined as the quest for the best health possible; and in fact, it's a positive goal achievable by everyone. Indeed, it's an actualization which every person can attain even though the true state of one's well-being depends upon his or her health potential. This concept can be stated in another way. Should a person have an illness, which only allows him to achieve a certain degree of well-being, then that desired level of good health becomes the highest attainment of well-being that's possible for the person. As such, good health becomes a biological-psychological "perfection" that mankind can achieve on Earth.

People attain good health by doing everything in their power to sustain their physical and mental well-being. To maintain good health people must obtain proper subsistence. They need to eat balanced meals and formulate diets which are nutritional. People have to protect themselves from the elements as well. They must avail themselves of protective wearing apparel by making sure they have warm clothing and adequate footwear. Also, people must strive to maintain their physical endurance, and in order to build up muscles and body strength, they should exercise on a daily basis. Additionally, people need to get adequate rest to allow their body to rejuvenate itself. They should also pursue social activities which promote psychological soundness. To help facilitate it, they should establish friendships which are meaningful and lasting. Similarly, they ought to involve themselves in relationships which bring about love and emotional security. Finally, people must seek out established medical services whenever they encounter threats to their well-being. In support of this, they should consult physicians, dentists, and other medical professionals on a regular basis. In summary, everyone must try to secure the best health care possible. And the way to ensure the most effective medical services remain available to people is to establish a universal institution of health care.

A universal system of health care would be structured according to the following design. There will be health care centers established in every major population region of a nation. Each center will consist of a complex of medical facilities dedicated to providing citizens with a broad spectrum of health care services

Health centers will provide care for every person in society. The health centers will provide service to all individuals regardless of age, sex, ethnic background, or race. The centers will serve everyone regardless of their economic status, religious convictions, or political beliefs.

The health centers will be staffed with administrators drawn from across the medical profession. There will be custodians, maintenance workers, and groundskeepers working at the centers. Receptionists, secretaries, and administrative clerks will be employed there as well.

The health centers will be staffed with interns, general practitioners, and doctors to treat patients with physical ailments. There will be brain surgeons, orthopedic specialists, dentists, and orthodontists as well. The centers will be staffed with medical assistants, laboratory technicians, and nurses. Additionally, there will be dietitians, physical therapists, and chiropractors. The centers will be staffed with psychoanalysts, psychologists, and psychiatrists to treat people with emotional and mental problems. The centers will be staffed with counselors for children and teenagers. Marriage and family counselors will be on call. The centers will have substance abuse counselors available as well. Further, the centers will be staffed with instructors on physical exercise, meditation, relaxation, and massage therapy. Basically, there will be specialists available at the health centers to aid anyone in need of medical attention.

The health care centers will provide care for all types of human illness. The health centers will provide treatment for every physical ailment ranging from headaches and sprained ankles to heart disease and cancer. Likewise, the centers will provide treatment for every mental ailment extending from anxiety and depression to nervous breakdowns and insanity. The centers will have access to the latest therapeutic and diagnostic technologies. They will be able to provide expertise at the highest level, i.e., the level available at the most advanced medical research facilities and schools of medicine.

The health centers will perform the services of a children's medical unit, a hospital, and a nursing home. The centers will provide the services available at a doctor's, dentist's, chiropractor's, and psychiatrist's office. The health care centers will house a pharmacy and medical equipment supply depot. The centers will further contain an exercise facility, gymnasium, and health spa. All necessary medical services will be centrally located and available at the health care centers.

The health care centers will provide medical equipment and supplies for all types of disorders. The health centers will provide ointments, salves, medicines, and drugs. The centers will provide vitamins, antibodies, and antitoxins. They will provide bandages. The centers will also provide corrective equipment such as eyeglasses, hearing aids, and dentures. They will provide canes, crutches, and wheelchairs. Additionally, the centers will provide heart pacemakers and artificial limbs.

The health care centers will provide analysis capabilities through the use of diagnostic equipment, which includes ultrasound, X-ray, NMR, PET and CAT-scan machines. The centers will have EKG equipment, blood analyzers, and so forth.

The health care centers will provide for various psychotherapy treatments. The health centers will provide treatment for drug dependency, including alcoholism, as well as treatment for the addiction to cocaine, heroin, etc. Additionally, the centers will provide inoculation programs to protect people against communicable diseases. The centers will provide first aid and ambulance services. The health care centers will also offer a poison control service. The centers will provide hospitalization for people who are injured and ill. Furthermore, the health care centers will provide complete care for the physically handicapped. In a similar fashion, they will provide psychological treatment for those who are emotionally or mentally challenged.

The health care centers will contain spas with whirlpool baths and saunas. There will be gymnasiums for all kinds of physical workouts. Exercise rooms will be equipped with apparatus like the treadmill, stationary bike, and weight-lift machine. Facilities will be provided for physiotherapy treatments including heat and light application, electrical stimulation, and body massage. In addition, there will be exercise programs set to music, such as aerobics, jazzercise, etc. The health centers will house basketball courts, badminton courts, squash courts, and tennis courts. At the health centers people will be able to participate in sports' activities such as volleyball, basketball, softball, baseball, and soccer.

The health care centers will establish educational programs on important health issues and concerns. The centers will offer education on every aspect of mental health. They will provide complete training on physical fitness as well. The centers will provide a series of diets adjusted for the people who have specified medical conditions, such as a vitamin deficiency or an allergy to certain food products. The health centers will instruct people on physical appearance, personal hygiene, and overall body care. People will be taught the benefits of adhering to a balanced diet, getting proper exercise, and obtaining adequate rest. They will be instructed on proper dental hygiene as well. People will learn about the physical and psychological problems associated with the abuse of drugs, alcohol, stimulants, and depressants.

The health centers will publish literature on current studies underway in the field of medical science. The centers will provide pamphlets on home safety and print instructions on how to avoid accidents and personal injury. The health centers will also offer courses on first-aid. Through training classes, people will be taught how to care for the physically handicapped. They will also learn how to provide assistance to the mentally challenged, emotionally impaired, etc.

People will be taught emergency evacuation procedures as well. They will learn how to mobilize themselves in times of national emergencies to adequately meet the crucial requirements of communication, transportation, shelter, and so forth. They will be taught how to secure, store, and then ration out the resources of food and water which are needed to survive. Hence, people will be taught how to respond to and survive the natural disasters of floods, forest fires, hurricanes, and earthquakes.

As discussed, the health care centers will provide for the diagnosis and treatment of every type of physical and mental illness. They will offer training and counseling on all health-related matters. The health care centers will provide medication. In addition, they will provide therapeutic and other corrective medical treatments. Importantly, the health care centers will also serve as research facilities. The facilities will be dedicated to studying the causes of illness as well as providing the medical resources needed to develop the cures for disease.

The health care centers will be facilities where both healthy and ill people can go. The centers will be staffed with instructors to conduct daily, weekly, and monthly exercise programs, which people would be encouraged to attend. Everyone would be encouraged to go to a health center on a regular basis, i.e., an hour or two every day, one or two nights a week, or three or four days a month. People would attend the centers to participate in exercise programs and sporting activities in order to maintain their well-being. At the health centers there would be social fulfillment as well, for the participants will be able interact with and enjoy the company of the other attendees.

There are two fundamental elements to the design of facilities belonging to the institution of health care. One element involves the facilities that are established for proactive purposes and are utilized by people to stay fit. This includes the indoor facilities with exercise rooms, gymnasiums, and swimming pools. It also includes the outdoor areas set aside for soccer fields, softball fields, and tennis courts. Activities at these facilities represent preventive care measures which people employ to avoid potential health problems. The other element involves the facilities that are intended to serve people for reactive reasons, i.e., to deal with after-the-fact medical conditions. These are the medical treatment facilities. They are built and staffed to address health problems which have arisen, been diagnosed, and are being treated. Such facilities include the first aid stations, doctor and dentist offices, medical clinics, hospitals, etc.

As it turns out, the preventive care facilities are a major component of both the institution of health care and recreation. Although health care and recreation are separate institutions, they are closely aligned in regard to their design to promote good health. Hence, they could share the same facilities, indoor and outdoor, when it comes to providing a place to exercise and participate in sporting activities.

The health centers would be funded through the employment sector of society. As described in the previous chapter, the universal employment institution provides people with the avenue to earn the basic necessities of life. In a similar fashion, people would work for a specific number of hours per week, weeks per year, or years out of their working career in order to pay for the health care system.

As with the other institutions of society, the health care system would not consist of public entities only. Like the employment structure, the health care system will contain privately owned and operated facilities. There will be doctors, dentists, etc., with their own practices. Likewise, there will be privately owned and operated hospitals, medical centers, nursing homes etc. Also there will be privately owned medical research labs, medical supply stores, pharmacies, ambulance services, and so forth. These independent medical providers would be encouraged to operate across society. They would offer all the medical services that the public system provides and will neither compete nor interfere with the universal institution of health care.

As we said, the goal of the universal institution of health care is to provide the best health care possible for every person alive. We might ask if it'll be easy for the universal institution of health care to attain this goal. The answer is it won't be easy; nonetheless, it is certainly achievable!

The gift of life is provided to everyone. Regardless of whether it turns out good or bad, the actualization of the gift is guaranteed to every person born. Good health, however, isn't guaranteed to anyone. As we know, an injury can disable a person for either a short period of time or permanently. An illness can disrupt one's life for a few days or for weeks, and a prolonged illness can prevent a person from being productive for months on end. Further, a major disease can debilitate an individual for the rest of his life.

For instance, a person can experience a disorder of the nervous system due to the misuse of drugs; and one can suffer damage to the brain, liver, or kidneys, as a result of the intake of toxins. Additionally, a lack of particular vitamins or nutrients in the diet can bring about a physical weakness. Furthermore, there are psychological threats to both the mind and body. We know that fear, frustration, and anger can bring on a serious emotional problem. Likewise, prolonged stress can cause depression and physical ailments as well.

Health, Education, Recreation

Human health is vulnerable to many threats. The threats may arise from an external source, or they may reside within the body. In any case, the threats must be overcome if the human race is to survive. The dangers to our well-being must be identified and researched, and the causes for physical and mental illnesses must be tracked down and eliminated. Such is the duty of the universal institution of health care.

Man must continue to make advances in health care through his experiment and research efforts. Scientists must synthesize new drugs in an attempt to cure disease; chemists must produce effective medicines to improve human health; and researchers must develop more nutritional foods in order to enhance physical strength and endurance. Similarly, medical specialists must proceed with the design and testing of new, artificial body parts. And likewise, the surgeons must continue to perform the necessary operations and organ transplants in an attempt to prolong life.

As man continues to do research in the field of medicine, however, he must take precautions not to contaminate the basic components of intracellular material. That is, he must ensure the drugs he develops won't result in long-term damage to the genetic structure of his species. Mankind is charged with improving the quality of life in the world without causing it irreversible harm.

The pursuit of good health is a never ending endeavor. Associated with the quest for good health is the desire to remain young. Throughout history, there's been an ongoing search for the "fountain of youth". Explorers have crossed oceans and seas, climbed mountains, and traversed jungles and deserts. People have searched for a "magic potion" which if found would keep them forever young. The explorers are still searching. However, their clothes have changed for they now wear white pants and lab jackets instead of coats of armor and heavy boots. Over the past several centuries, their travels have taken them away from the mountain tops and into the research laboratories. Today's explorers are the medical scientists who work with test tubes and Petri dishes. The scientists study DNA and cellular metabolism. They study the human biological life processes. These scientists study the aging process and the causes of natural death. Medical scientists attempt to regulate the metabolic functions with the goal of preventing our body's cells, tissues, and organs from deteriorating as rapidly as they do.

The scientists work to eliminate harmful bacteria and viruses throughout the world. Doctors cure diseases and illnesses, whereas surgeons perform operations and organ transplants. In the medical field there are researchers who strive to postpone the onset of death. We note, however, that researchers don't try to eliminate death. We cannot prevent death from happening, for it's the natural conclusion to the human experience on Earth. It occurs when the forces in Nature which tear down the human body eventually surpass the forces that try to build and maintain it.

Although the human species cannot prevent the occurrence of death, it can work to prevent premature death. Mankind can help avoid unexpected death due to injury or accident. And people can try to prevent premature death because of illness or disease. Through a commitment to the universal institution of health care, human beings can attempt to prevent early and unnecessary death.

The species of man must promote the positive achievements made in the field of health care. People should stress the need to get proper nutrition, sufficient exercise, and adequate rest. Likewise, they should emphasize the importance of obtaining appropriate medical care when needed. People must work to eliminate any unsafe conditions at home and in the work place. Further, they must strive to eliminate the health risks found within the environment such as pollutants, carcinogens, man-generated radioactivity, etc.

The major objective of the universal institution of health care is to eliminate all illnesses, physical and mental. The aim is to have everyone stay as healthy as he or she possibly can. In this endeavor, the universal institution of health care will utilize the best medical treatment and technology known to man. The goal then is to have as many people live as long as possible, with as little physical and mental discomfort as possible.

Another major institution of mankind is the universal institution of education. We said a person should have the opportunity to work in an occupation of his choice. We further indicated it should include the chance to work in an occupation which holds one's interest. Before he can do this, however, a person has to decide where his interests lie. In addition, he has to have knowledge of his abilities as it pertains to his mental and physical attributes. In other words, an individual must discover where his potential lies within a specific field of employment.

Education is the conduit an individual utilizes to prepare himself for a career. A person must be educated to perform well in any field of endeavor; and the means to gain the skills necessary to perform well is afforded through the institution of education.

Health, Education, Recreation

As mentioned, prior to working in an occupation of choice, a person must first prepare himself. Everyone needs the proper training and everyone must develop the basic skills. Each person must attain the degree of competence that's needed to do a good job. The attainment of the competency and necessary skills comes about early in life, and to a large extent, it occurs during childhood and the adolescence years.

Across the world, parents help their children develop into contributing members of society. They do so through the process of education. To start with, they teach their children to walk and talk, as well as to read and write. People also teach their children how to survive in the world. That is, they teach them to hunt and fish. Likewise, they teach them to cook and sew. They also teach their children how to manage a farm which can involve the tasks of plowing, planting, and working the fields. They teach them the skills of the trades such as plumbing, masonry, electrical work, and carpentry. People teach their children social skills as well. They teach them how to interact with others and gain the acceptance of their peers. People also teach children the skills of fine workmanship. Similarly, they teach them how to develop their talents in music, dance, and art. Within the school environment, educators teach children the fundamentals of math. They teach them geometry, algebra, and calculus. Educators also instruct children on the natural sciences including biology, chemistry, and physics. The teachers further instruct children on the social sciences such as sociology and psychology. They further teach them philosophy, history, and religion. To prepare for entry into the workforce, adults teach young people the principles of economics. To prepare for good citizenship, the adults teach children the principles of government and law.

Education indeed is important because it teaches young people how to live in a social world. As indicated, adults provide children with a vast amount of knowledge during their formative years. Adults provide them with a tremendous amount of scientific and technical data. Also, they give them a considerable amount of instruction dealing with moral responsibility and social behavior. In a similar fashion, adults instruct children on current or approved work ethics and ways to improve their station in life. Throughout history, there will always be the need to educate young people on how to function satisfactory in a social environment.

The institution of education serves man's social design in a number of important ways. On a broad level, education helps groups of citizens meet the requirements for successful social living. Some examples of this are the following. On-the-job training instructs the factory employees on ways to be more productive in the workplace. Published literature on product quality and safety standards informs the consumers on how to better evaluate goods and services in the marketplace. Likewise, instruction on the rules of law informs the citizens on the importance of personal accountability and the consequences of misbehavior.

The institution of education helps instill moral values and acceptable patterns of behavior. As indicated, it instructs young people on how to become law-abiding members of society. In a similar manner, it helps adults learn how to be good parents. A well-founded educational system then develops responsible citizens across the entire age spectrum, and in meeting this challenge, it helps keep the social structure intact.

Education also serves society on a personal level for it helps a person mature psychologically. Education is a key facilitator which allows an individual to develop his intellectual capabilities. A person learns facts, formulates concepts, and expands his cognitive skills. Education is also a tool that helps an individual mature emotionally. It encourages a person to establish goals, and when the goals aren't met, it instructs one on how to handle disappointment. Furthermore, education promotes self-assuredness. Indeed, a supportive and well-designed educational system helps an individual become more secure as he strives to meet the potentials of his mind.

As discussed earlier, a key function of the educational process is to help a person prepare for an occupation. It allows an individual to acquire sufficient knowledge so he can enter a field which meets his interests. Hence, education provides the training a person needs to successfully pursue a career of his or her choosing.

Another key function of the educational process is to present knowledge to everyone who can benefit from it. Hence, educational opportunities must be available to every member of society from young children to grown adults. Instructional training must be provided to all citizens from teenagers to the senior citizens.

Education then produces and disseminates information useful to all sectors of society. For example, education instructs people on ways to prepare food, mend clothing, make home repairs, and so forth. Likewise, it instructs people on how to shop, operate a personal computer, service an automobile, etc. Further, education helps people become more competent in the workplace. Training at work helps employees become effective in resolving problems and completing their job assignments. Another responsibility of the educational system is to teach people the advantages of maintaining good health. It instructs people on the importance of personal hygiene, adequate nutrition, proper exercise, etc.

Without question, another highly important function of the educational system is to advance the other institutions of society. It meets this responsibility in a variety of ways, some of which include the following. Education serves as the avenue utilized by academia to teach the principles of economics. It is the means used by law enforcement to provide instruction on the rules of proper conduct. It is also the conduit employed by ecclesiastical authorities to promote the moral doctrines sanctioned by religion. Overall, education is the mechanism that's employed by generation after generation of human beings as they strive to maintain social stability and secure their place in history. Indeed, the institution of education is the pathway that serves to promote and preserve our entire cultural heritage.

The role of the institution of education then is to satisfy the several duties we've outlined above. In order to accomplish this, the universal institution of education ought to be structured in the following way.

The universal institution of education would consist of a vast network of learning centers that provide instruction to citizens on ways to live and work constructively in a social environment. The universal educational system would provide the opportunity for training to everyone no matter what his or her age, sex, race, or ethnic background. It would provide the opportunity for training regardless of one's political opinions or religious beliefs. It would provide opportunity for training regardless of one's socioeconomic status.

A universal educational system will encompass the duties of the nursery schools, day care centers, elementary schools, junior high schools and high schools. It'll take on the responsibilities of the colleges and universities. It will also take on the functions of the trade schools and job schools normally associated with business and industry. In conjunction with the institution of discovery, the universal institution of education will assume the tasks and services currently provided by the libraries and museums.

The universal institution of education would consist of several divisions which are structured according to subject matter and areas of technology. There will be divisions for all the major fields of natural science. There will be divisions for business and industry as well. There will be divisions based upon crafts and trades, communication and transportation, agriculture and the environment. The social sciences will have representative divisions including divisions for the humanities and arts. The administration of all the major divisions of the institution of education will be centrally located.

The division for the natural sciences will include separate units on biology, chemistry, and physics. There will also be a unit on geology. There will be a unit on mathematics as well.

Another division of the educational institution will involve space technology. This division will offer courses of study on the macrocosm and include units on astronomy and space exploration. Scientific information relating to the planets, stars, and galaxies will be collected as well as data on the forces and events occurring across the universe. Knowledge pertaining to the transposition of life processes from the earth to a space environment will be learned.

There will be a division for energy. This covers the resources of fossil fuel including coal, oil, and natural gas. It covers the supplies of energy which are provided by wind power, hydroelectric power, and solar radiation. It covers the nuclear sources of energy as well. The units within the energy division will provide information on the uses and misuses of energy. They will likewise provide literature on the conservation and storage of energy. They will offer training courses on the acquisition, distribution, and utilization of energy. They will provide instruction on disposal of nuclear waste materials as well.

There will be a division for electrical science. This will consist of units on various applications of electronic-based technologies. This includes a unit on equipment for data processing such as computers and process control devices. It includes a unit on equipment in the medical field such as devices for electrocardiographic monitoring as well as electromyographic diagnosis. It includes medical equipment for electroconvulsive therapy and electrotherapeutic treatments. It includes equipment for biological applications such as the devices developed for electro-osmosis and electrotonics. Also, there will be units focused on associated technologies including electro-optic, electromagnetic, electro-thermal and electromechanical applications.

There will be a division for medical science. This will include health care and pharmaceutical units. It will house dental and doctoral units as well as units on therapeutic and surgical procedures. It will contain units that pertain to psychoanalysis and psychotherapy. It'll also contain units on first aid, physical therapy, and chiropractics.

There will be a division for the building trades. The construction division will be comprised of separate units on architecture and structural engineering. There will be units on masonry, carpentry, electrical wiring, and plumbing. Also, there will be a unit dedicated to the maintenance and repair of buildings.

There will also be a division for business and industry. It will include units on the manufacturing process, distribution of merchandise, and inventory management. It'll include units on trade and commerce. It will also consist of units on the advertisement, sale, and marketing of product. Further, it will contain training units designated for people in managerial, clerical, and secretarial positions.

There will be a division for communication. The communication division will have units that house telephone and telegraph services. It'll contain units that are associated with the electronic transmission of information via computers, fax machines, and so forth. There will also be units that deal with the transmission of radio and television signals via broadcast towers, space satellites, etc.

There will be a division for transportation. This division will have units on the transport of raw materials, component parts, and manufactured products that are shipped through the mediums of land, sea, or air. The units cover various means of travel that range from single passenger vehicles to mass transportation systems. The units will offer programs on the maintenance of privately-owned vehicles, such as the motorcycle and automobile. Likewise, the units will provide information on the successful operation of transit systems that utilize multi-person carriers like the bus, train, ship, and airliner.

There will be a division for the social sciences. This division will include units on psychology, sociology, and economics. There will be units on civics, ethics, and philosophy. Also, there will be units on government, religion, history, etc.

There will be a division for the fine arts. It will include units designated for language, music, dance, and song. It will include drawing, painting, and sculpturing units as well.

There will be a division for agriculture. This will include units which relate to the food sources of livestock, poultry, and fish. It'll include units on the operations of beef cattle ranches as well as dairy farms. It'll include units on the management of fruit orchards, vegetable fields, and lands set aside for grain crops. It will also include units which provide information to citizens on such subjects as food supplements, vitamins, nutrition, etc.

There will be a division for the environment. It will cover the state of the world's air, soil, and water supplies. The division's role will be to collect and distribute factual information which pertains to the world's ecosystems. It will provide instruction on ways to prevent pollution, erosion, and the waste of natural resources. Overall, it'll function to restore and maintain a high level of stability to the world's major environments.

Another division of the institution of education will be dedicated to information management. It will involve the collection, transfer, and processing of data. It'll also handle the storage and retrieval of information. The division's work will encompass reference material and technical reports from research studies. It will further ensure that scientific records and historical documents are preserved. There will be printing and publishing facilities located in this unit. In association with the universal institution of discovery, the data management division will be home to the libraries, museums, and archive buildings.

Where appropriate, these educational divisions and their corresponding units will interface directly with the managerial boards of the several universal institutions of society. Thereby, the educational curriculum that's being presented to the citizens would be aligned with the objectives and needs of the key sectors of societal life including health care, communication, transportation, energy, and so forth.

Further, each organizational division of education would be functionally associated with a major learning center of society. Each learning center would be structurally designed according to the segment of the population which it serves. That is, there will be separate learning centers for youth, college-age students, working people, etc. Each learning center will administer its own programs in regard to curriculums, methods of training, staff size and responsibilities. There will be several learning centers established within each community wherein the centers may or may not be housed in the same building complex.

The learning centers are public training complexes and part of the universal institution of education. In many ways, they are similar in design to the public school systems of today. The instructors will be professional educators who have teaching as their full time responsibility. The learning centers would be funded through the universal institution of employment in the same manner as other major institutions like health care and recreation. The learning centers will be managed by professional administrators.

Each learning center would provide instructorship to a designated segment of society. One learning center will involve the training of pre-school-age children, thereby providing educational opportunities for youngsters below six years of age. It will encompass the duties which are now performed in pre-school, nursery school, and day care facilities. The youngsters will be taught basic skills in language and math, and introduced to the fundamental principles of science. On a broader scale, they will be given instruction pertaining to human culture and history. Through classroom activities in artistry and drawing, the young people will develop their capabilities of perception and creativity. And through activities on the playground, the youngsters' abilities of coordination, strength, and agility will be enhanced. Additionally, the youngsters will be taught the social skills of communication and cooperation. Also, they will be taught the importance of discipline and personal accountability. Young people will also be instructed on the value of accomplishment. The youngsters in this learning center would be provided encouragement for their efforts and reinforcement for their accomplishments. There would be emphasis placed upon building the children's self-esteem. Overall, the youngsters will be given the fundamental tools needed to learn and grow in a social environment.

Another learning center will involve the elementary school-age children. This center will serve the educational needs of children in grades one through six. The learning center will provide for educational opportunities which are now being performed in the public and private school systems.

The same would be true for a third learning center that provides educational opportunities for the junior and senior high school students. This center would be designed to meet the needs of young people in grades seven through twelve.

A fourth learning center will be structured to correspond to the college-age level. This center will offer fields of study in the social and natural sciences. The social science emphasis would be upon general studies in literature, philosophy, psychology, sociology, government, history, etc. Also, it will offer study programs in the areas of mathematics and the natural sciences of geology, biology, chemistry, physics, etc. The curriculums would be broadly based with subject matter presented in the framework of an overview. The courses of study at this learning center would extend from two to six years with degree programs set up at two-year intervals. Over the six year program there would be three graduation levels of accomplishment.

Associated with the fourth learning center will be highly specialized programs within each field of study. A fifth learning center would administer these in-depth study programs. The in-depth programs will be available to students who wanted to study exclusively in a single field such as medicine, biology, chemistry, physics, mathematics, banking, economics, law, history, sociology, psychology, etc. As indicated, this learning center will offer complete programs of instruction for every field of natural and social science. The degree program would extend from two to eight years. Again the programs would be set up at two-year increments, meaning over an eight year span, there would be four degree levels which a person could earn. The participants will be declared eligible for graduation at each level, once they complete the specified training in their respective field of study. The candidates will be required to give an oral-presentation on the subject matter as well as pass a written examination. They will also have to demonstrate "hands-on" skills by completing a specified internship at a participating enterprise within their major field of study.

To be certified in a profession, the potential graduates would have to demonstrate an acceptable level of competence in their designated career field. There will be considerable flexibility in regard to becoming certified within the different fields of study. Some programs would require completion of six years at general studies level and some would require completion of eight years at the in-depth studies level. However, for the majority of programs, the candidates could be certified following the completion of a total of four to eight years study, at various combinations of the general studies and in-depth studies programs.

A sixth learning center would be comprised of the occupational and trade schools. The fundamentals of service-orientated occupations will be taught at this learning center. The job skills of a bus driver, auto mechanic, and appliance repairman will be taught. Job skills of a construction worker and shipbuilder will be taught as well. The job skills of an electrician, plumber, carpenter, and bricklayer will be taught. The job skills of a butcher, baker, and chef will also be taught. People could learn to become a computer programmer, software installer, or repairman of printers and copiers. People could learn to become a conservation officer or forester. They could be taught the job requirements of a gardener or groundskeeper. The job skills of a manicurist, cosmetician, and hairdresser will be taught.

The competencies of a dietetic advisor, sports trainer, and nurse's aid will be taught as well. Also, the job skills of a secretary, salesperson, and fashion model will be taught.

This learning center would be closely aligned with the business and industry sector of society. Its instructional programs would be designed to serve the needs of the entire working community. Its function would be to train people for all occupations in the employment structure that don't require a college degree or professional certification. In many cases, this learning center will focus on jobs that provide support to other highly technical and professional positions. The workers who want to upgrade job skills in their present occupation will be given the opportunity through this learning center. Likewise, the workers who wish to learn the skills of a new occupation could do so.

A seventh learning center will involve training in the arts and crafts. It will also include instructorship on skills that are useful to everyday living. Basically, it would provide studies on subject matters of current interest to society. This learning center will consist of a network of schools dedicated to specialized talents and skills, and operate similar to the continuing education programs that are now in place at many high schools and colleges. In the area of arts and crafts, the learning center will offer courses in drawing, painting, and sculpturing. It will offer courses in acting, dance, and music. Also, it will offer courses in woodworking, glass blowing, pottery, weaving, etc.

In the arena of useful, everyday skills this learning center will offer courses in electrical wiring, soldering, and small appliance repair. It will offer courses in home gardening and auto maintenance. It will offer courses in varnishing, plastering, and wall papering. The learning center will also offer courses in sewing, tailoring, and shoe repair. The center will offer courses in cooking, baking, cake decorating, etc. It'll offer courses in typing and computer data entry. Further, it will offer courses in writing and public speaking. The training provided at the seventh learning center will be available to all members of society.

An eighth learning center would be designed to meet the day-to-day societal needs of adults. This eighth center will provide training of a practical nature and involve activities that apply to everyday situations such as pursuit of employment, shopping, and household management. The courses will be for a short duration where most periods of instruction would last but a few hours. This learning center will publish pamphlets and literature on an assortment of topics that deal with the responsibilities and tasks of everyday life. Some examples of the services to be provided at this learning center are the following.

In the area of job procurement, this center will offer courses on how to write a resume, complete a job application form, and present oneself at an interview. For business management, it will offer courses on how to fill out performance appraisals, conduct a meeting, present data, etc. In the personal finance area, the center will offer courses on how to balance a checkbook, maintain a budget, etc. In the area of financial investment, the center will offer courses on how to purchase stocks and bonds, establish trust funds, and manage an estate. In consumer marketing, the center will offer courses on how to shop for bargains, purchase major appliances, and evaluate the quality of manufactured goods. Relative to the role of being a parent, the center will offer courses on how to administer discipline, deal with unruly teenagers, and so forth. The parenting courses will further place emphasize on ways to enhance a child's self-esteem. In the area of family living, people will be instructed on how to secure a home mortgage, save for their children's college costs, and plan a vacation. Additionally, in regard to involvement with youth sports, there will be training classes on how to coach a team in soccer, basketball, baseball, or football. In the senior citizen realm, there will be instructorship on how to live on a fixed income, prepare a will, secure investments for one's heirs, etc. This learning center then will provide training for all people in all facets of social living.

The universal institution of education will be managed by professional educators. They'll be administrators with a strong business and education background. All the learning centers will be staffed with instructors and teachers drawn from various sectors of society. The employment sector, for example, will provide technical experts as needed for each discipline or field of study. Similarly, the occupational and trade school centers will rely upon businesses and industries to provide their source of instructorship.

The nursery school learning centers will be staffed with certified teachers. The nursery school centers would also be supported by parents and other adults committed to the development of pre-school age children. The learning centers designated for students from the elementary school level through the college level will be staffed with career educators. Additionally, the adult education centers will be staffed with instructors who hold special skills and talents. Such instructors will include accountants, financial advisors, and family counselors, as well as artisans and craftsmen. Additionally, the libraries and museums will be staffed with qualified educators.

The learning centers will employ people from society at large. Many elderly and retired people will be able to work part-time in libraries, archive buildings, and museums. This would provide the elderly with the opportunity to be productive and contribute to the educational development of young people who visit these facilities. The learning centers will also be staffed by parents and other adults who are willing to volunteer their time and expertise. Needless to say, the instructors employed in all of the learning centers ought to be individuals who enjoy teaching. They should be educators who gain satisfaction in expanding the learning horizons of the people they instruct.

As we know, success in the employment world depends to a large extent upon a person's educational background. Not unexpectedly, the education institution is closely linked to the institution of employment. To pay for one's educational expenses, a person could work in the universal employment institution according to one of the following schedule-designs. That is, a person works a certain number of hours per week, a certain number of weeks per year, or a certain number of years out of his employable career. A possible scenario would have the person working for two to five years in a public service job. The public service job could be in the field of medicine or health care. An individual might work in a nursing home, a dental clinic, a hospital, etc. Similarly, the job could be in the realm of governmental service. The person might serve in the military or the police department. Possibly he could work in the postal service. Additionally, the job could be in the field of transportation or communication. Likewise, the job could be in the area of aeronautics or space science. It could be in the field of energy where one works for a utility company. The job could be in the field of agriculture, lumber, or mining. It could be in the construction trades as well. Further, the job could be in the environmental field wherein a person works in a state or national park.

A young adult can go to school and work part-time in any public service position to finance the costs of his education. Just as with the housing, food, clothing, and health care benefits, the educational allowance would be earned by working a specified period of time. There would be an open enrollment to work in the universal institution of employment, available to anyone who wishes to avail himself of the educational amenities that it provides.

Just as the private businesses and industries are encouraged across society, so the private and parochial schools will continue to operate. All levels of privately owned and operated schools, ranging from nursery schools to trade schools to the universities, would be promoted in society. The private educational facilities would be available for those individuals who didn't wish to participate in the universal institution of education.

There are two catalysts of key significance to the entire educational process. One is the profession of the teacher. A teacher is instrumental in helping to develop the interests and skills of a young person. The other catalyst is the parent. The parent's role in nurturing a child's intellectual and emotional growth is exceedingly important. The parent and teacher have the responsibility to establish a positive learning environment at home and in the school.

Both parent and teacher serve as positive role models. They set the personal standards for children to follow in regards to proper behavior. The parent and teacher offer guidance and discipline. They also instill social values and moral beliefs. Further, the parent and teacher help young people study and learn about the world. The parent and teacher instruct children on ways to develop their talents and pursue their interests. Finally, both the parent and teacher instruct young people on how to establish worthwhile goals in life.

Mankind has always sought happiness in life. Happiness is attainable and its pursuit is a worthwhile endeavor. This brings us to another major institution of mankind, the institution of recreation.

People seek enjoyment through entertainment and sports. Enjoyment in life can be attained, and its realization is the goal of the institution of recreation. Recreation is perhaps the least structured institution in society today. Nonetheless, it's an institution that's very important to the physical and psychological well-being of man.

The institution of recreation encompasses all forms of entertainment. It includes listening to the radio and watching television. It includes going to the movies. It includes attending plays, concerts, and operas. It includes reading books as well. It includes playing card games such as hearts, canasta and fan tan. It includes playing board games like Monopoly, Parcheesi, and Sorry. Similarly, it includes playing video games on the computer.

The institution of recreation includes all forms of controlled (legalized) gambling activities. It includes those involved with betting on horse racing, dog racing, etc. It also includes those associated with casino operations. Casino operations take in the card table games of blackjack, baccarat, Texas hold'em, and pai gow poker. They also take in the non-card table games like the roulette wheel and the dice game of craps. Also included are the slot machines, including video poker, let-it-ride, and regular slots. Other gambling activities include the numbers games of bingo, keno, and lotto.

The institution of recreation involves all kinds of leisure-time activities. It includes dancing and bowling, as well as bicycling and roller-skating. It includes swimming, boating, and jet skiing. It includes hunting and fishing. It also includes skydiving.

The institution of recreation consists of all types of sporting activities. It consists of playing badminton and croquet, as well as playing tennis and golf. It also consists of archery and trap shooting. The institution of recreation includes motorcycling and auto racing. It also includes cross-country and downhill skiing. Further, the institution of recreation covers all organized team sports. This includes basketball, baseball, and football. It also includes ice hockey, soccer, and lacrosse.

The institution of recreation further consists of outdoor activities such as picnics and reunions. It consists of walks in parks, hiking, and camping. The institution of recreation also involves games and rides that are featured at carnivals, circuses, and amusement parks.

Of the major institutions in society, the institution of recreation is least organized as a formal institution. Not surprisingly, it is also an institution that's had minimal emphasis placed upon it relative to its role in society. Let's look at some factors that have positioned recreation to where it is in the hierarchy of institutional priorities.

An important reason for recreation's lower priority has been due to world economics. Historically, the world's social-economic systems have required people to work for long hours at physically demanding jobs. In the past, people worked the entire day to provide the basic necessities of food, clothing, and shelter. People had neither the time nor the energy to seek out forms of entertainment on a consistent basis. Furthermore, the vast majority of people didn't have the money to pay for the entertainment opportunities which did exist. Only recently have entrepreneurs been able to establish major venues for sports and other recreational events on a broad scale. Only recently has the entertainment industry become a significant ingredient in the cultural development of man.

Another major reason why the institution of recreation had less emphasis placed upon it is because of the placement of values. Over the centuries, people were conditioned to believe that working is more important than enjoying life. People were taught that hard work is, in and of itself, a rewarding and satisfying experience. Indeed, modern-day work ethics instruct people to work first and enjoy life later.

Without question, the desire to apply oneself to his or her profession is a desirable human trait. A reinforcement of this view is the fact that no person feels badly if he works too much. No one feels guilty if he puts in a difficult day on the job. Actually, everyone is rewarded in a psychological sense if he feels he has expended his physical or mental capabilities while performing on the job. A good illustration of work-based, self-fulfillment is seen in many, highly focused individuals who own and operate their own businesses.

The same feelings of self-worth come about when one works for a charitable cause. No person feels negligent if he devotes a significant amount of time to a charitable organization. For example, no one feels guilty if he is highly committed to a church benevolence group. Likewise, no one feels guilty if he is deeply involved in a volunteer fire company or a hometown ambulance service. Indeed, one prides himself in how hard he works in such an endeavor. Thus, a person prides himself in how many hours he's able to dedicate to the success of a worthwhile project.

On the other hand, nearly everyone feels guilty if he spends too much time in leisure-time activities. Sooner or later, everyone feels guilty if he is having an excessive amount of fun. On occasion, a person feels he's wasting his time if he becomes too involved in recreational pursuits. That is, a person may feel he wastes his time if he watches several hours of television a night. A person might think he squanders too much time if he sunbathes all afternoon on the beach. Similarly, he may feel he wastes his time if spends a week or two fishing, or a month reading a dozen or more novels. Likewise, a person may think he's wasting part of his life if he spends several months participating in a sports activity such as bowling or golf. Additionally, a person might feel he's wasting his life if he spends years in the pursuit of a hobby like painting or stamp collecting.

The truth is a person isn't wasting his time! Life is to be enjoyed. A fundamental privilege for being alive is to be able to enjoy it. Indeed, a person can work hard and enjoy life. As a matter of fact, a person is alive to pursue both of these endeavors.

In recent times, recreation has emerged as an important institution of mankind. One factor which brought recreation to the forefront has to do with the onslaught of technological advances made in the twentieth century. A number of components found within the institution of recreation are new. Many of them arose in the fields of communication and transportation. We know the invention of the telephone, radio, and television set are recent advances in the field of communication. So too are the motion picture, video tape, e-mail via computer, and electronic transmission from space-based satellites. In regard to transportation, the introduction of motorized means of travel have made it possible for people to take day trips for sightseeing, as well as schedule month-long excursions to distant resorts. From a historical standpoint, the automobile, train, cruise ship and airplane are relatively new types of transportation.

Another key reason for the shift of emphasis on recreation has been due to the consolidation of amateur sports into formalized professional enterprises. Only recently have organized sports become major components of the entertainment business. As we know, sports such as tennis, basketball, baseball, football, and soccer have captured the interest of people on a world-wide basis. For the most part, admissions to professional sport competitions are affordable, and sporting contests are attended on an annual basis by millions upon millions of people.

It is important then for every person to be happy and enjoy life. It's important for everyone to have fun and pursue leisure time activities. A key advantage to the restructured employment institution described in chapter 6 is the elimination of the need for worry; that is, the worry people have about not accomplishing something worthwhile in life. People wouldn't have to worry that they don't contribute enough time or resources to a charitable organization. Instead, their life-contributions will already have been taken care of. The universal employment structure we've outlined will meet the philanthropic needs of society. When a person leaves work at the end of the day, he can be satisfied he's accomplished something worthwhile. Thus, he can be at ease and enjoy his time away from the job. A person will be content because he'll know his work on the job meets the humanitarian requirements of mankind.

In a restructured employment institution, a person will be able to satisfy both his need to work and the desire to be at peace with himself. While working on the job, every individual will know he's accomplishing a worthwhile goal in providing a product or service useful to society. In the same light, he'll be able to relax while not working and truly enjoy life. A person will be able to enjoy his family and friends. He'll be able to participate in leisure-time activities with family and friends such as bowling, golfing, hiking, and camping. He'll be able to participate in these activities without the concern of being non-contributive to the advancement social living.

At this point, let's describe how the universal institution of recreation might be structured. The universal institution of recreation would be organized into a series of sport-exercise-entertainment complexes. There would be recreational complexes built in each community with all types of entertainment and recreational activities available. The design would be similar to the health centers and sports complexes which are seen in many of today's societies.

The recreation centers will contain theaters for movies as well as stages for musicals and plays. There will also be auditoriums for concerts and operas. The centers will contain gymnasiums for activities such as badminton, volleyball, and basketball. There will be exercise rooms and facilities for saunas, whirlpools, etc. The recreation centers will house billiard rooms and bowling lanes. There will be roller skate and ice skate rinks. In addition, the centers will contain a swimming pool plus a ballroom for dance. The centers will also have a rifle and pistol range for target shooting.

The centers will provide areas for table tennis and shuffleboard. There will be places set aside for electronic and video games. There will be rooms for playing cards and board games like Monopoly, Sorry, Parcheesi, Clue, and Trivia Pursuit. The recreation centers will have facilities for the arts and crafts as well. People will be able to learn skills in photography. They will be able to take instruction in artistry and learn how to paint portraits, still life, and landscapes. People will be able to learn how to sew and weave as well as do latch hook and macramé.

The recreation centers will also house an amusement park. There will be mechanical rides and games of chance, which are normally associated with circuses, carnivals, and county fairs. There will be roller coaster rides, Ferris wheels, merry-go-rounds, water slides, and so on.

The recreation centers will have outdoor facilities for sports including baseball, softball, football, and soccer. There will be tennis and squash courts. There will be picnic areas as well. The centers will have areas set aside for horseback riding and golfing. There will also be trails designated

Health, Education, Recreation   127

for biking, hiking, and jogging. There will be parklands with wooded areas designated for camping in the summertime. Likewise, the parklands will contain cleared hillsides that are groomed for sledding and skiing in the winter.

The recreation centers would provide the opportunity for relaxation and enjoyment for all citizens. The centers would be open to everyone in society and people could go there as they pleased on a daily, weekly, or monthly basis.

The institution of recreation will be managed by professional administrators. The administrators' job would deal with the development and implementation of broad-based recreational programs. Their responsibilities would further include the construction and operation of state-of-the-art sports facilities. Overall, the managers would focus on promoting the well-being and happiness of all citizens through participation in sports and recreation.

As in the case of the institutions of health care and education, the universal institution of recreation would be funded through participation in the employment sector of society. The universal employment institution would support recreation in the same manner it supports other important areas of human endeavor, i.e., education, health care, and the basic needs of food, clothing, and shelter. People would work a specified number of hours per week, a specified number of weeks per year, or a specified number of years during their working career in order to pay for the amenities offered via the recreational institution.

Privately-owned recreation enterprises would be encouraged throughout society as well. The establishment of the non-public facilities for sports and entertainment purposes would serve as an important resource in meeting society's recreational needs. These facilities will include theaters, convention centers, and concert halls. They will include swimming pools, gymnasiums, sports stadiums, and fields of play. The privately owned and operated facilities would not compete with the universal institution of recreation. In fact, many of the people who operate the facilities in the universal institution of recreation would be drawn from the private sector of society.

In addition, the privately-owned recreation enterprises would sanction professional sports leagues. They would establish teams to complete against each other, and appropriately, they'd field professional athletes to play on the teams. This would be along the same lines as the professional sports' leagues of today. Current examples of professional sport organizations include the soccer leagues of Europe, the hockey leagues of Canada, and the baseball leagues of the United States of America.

Hence, everyone should have avenues open to secure a well-rounded education, excellent health care, and the chance to experience a happy life. If society is structured as we've outlined in preceding chapters, the results of man's labor will automatically fulfill his purpose in life. And if the universal employment institution functions as we've described, everyone will have the opportunity to work in an occupation that contributes to the advancement of social living.

8

Requisite Institutions

WE CAN GROUP THE institutions of mankind into several key categories depending on the function they perform. One category deals with a person's growth and development. It is associated with the influence of one's parents, siblings, and other relatives. This is represented by the institution of the family which we describe in chapter 3. Another category relates to social behavior with a moral bias. This involves the institutions of religion and government which are discussed in chapters 4 and 5 respectively. A third category deals with the survival needs of man and is covered by the institution of employment. Employment provides the means to earn a living and satisfy man's requirement for food, clothing, and shelter. It is the topic of chapter 6. Another survival need is health care and this institution is described in chapter 7. A fourth category involves two significant endeavors which contribute to the general well-being of man. One involves learning and training and is the responsibility of the institution of education. The other involves rest and relaxation and falls under the auspices of the institution of recreation. Both the educational and recreational institutions are also discussed in chapter 7.

A fifth category involves human accessibility. It's represented by the institutions of communication and transportation. A sixth category involves the means citizens employ to meet financial concerns. It's involved with banking and covers lending services and savings opportunities which the banks provide. It is labeled the institution of financial resource. A seventh category involves the acquisition and distribution of resources that are essential for human living. This category involves the institutions of utility-service and energy. The institution of ecology represents an eighth category. It covers the world's eco-systems and appropriately takes in man's interactions with the plant and animal communities. A ninth category involves the environment itself, i.e., the non-living world. A tenth category involves cultural advancement and preservation and is labeled the institution of discovery. The discovery institution deals with knowledge and involves new compositions of matter as well as new ways to improve social living. Libraries and museums, which are established to secure advancements in modern-day living, are included in this institution.

In the preceding chapters we discussed the institutions of family, religion, government, employment, health, education, and recreation. In this chapter we discuss the latter institutions identified above. They are the institutions of communication, transportation, financial resource, utilities-service, and energy. They also include the institutions of ecology, environment, and discovery. Together, we label them as the institutions of human requisite. They are pertinent to the activities and services needed to live successfully in a social environment.

A universal institution of communication should be established within society. The institution would consist of a nationwide network of communication centers containing telephone companies, radio broadcasters, and television stations. It would contain a public-based internet service as well. It would house an assemblage of printing and publishing facilities and a network of magazine, journal, and book publishing houses. It would also be home to a conglomeration of daily and weekly newspapers. The conglomeration would consist of a broad-based alignment of newspaper editors, printers, publishers, and distributors. The communication institution would further include telegraph, teletype, and fax services. It would include space-based satellites and other transmission facilities.

Further, the communication institution would contain a nationwide postal system for the delivery of mail by means of truck, train, ocean vessel, and airplane. All forms of mail delivery from electronic mailing and fax copies to hard copy mailing will be provided. All items from postcards and letters to large packages will be handled. This national postal service will have offices and distribution centers located in every community, thereby providing a coordinated system to effectively move mail, packages, etc., across the various elements of society.

The universal institution of communication would oversee the dissemination of information via every available media and ensure that important matters are communicated to the appropriate segments of the population. Basically, the information disseminated would be useful to the day-to-day operations of the other institutions of society. For instance, there will be publications on issuances of governmental regulations as well as recent court decisions. There will be publications on new advances in medicine, nutrition, and health care. Also, there will be publications relating to current transportation conditions. There will be releases regarding new technologies developed through scientific research, as well as transmissions on issues of the day whether it involved energy utilization, environmental concerns, or safety in the workplace. Further, there will be broadcasts on matters of local interest such as current employment opportunities, ongoing recreational programs, and upcoming social events. The coordinated distribution of information would well serve the several institutions and citizenry of society.

The universal institution of communication will be governed by a managerial board comprised of executives chosen from participating communication companies. The members of the managerial board will be elected for pre-determined lengths of service.

In addition to the universal institution of communication, there would be private enterprises established throughout the communication field. They would include privately-owned newspapers, book publishers, and radio and television stations. They would also include independently owned and operated mail delivery and postal services. The private companies would not compete with the broadcast entities belonging to the universal communication institution. Rather, they would function alongside the public sector to satisfy the general communicational needs of society.

There should be established a universal institution of transportation. This institution would consist of a broad network of transportation facilities and services. It would provide for the delivery of raw materials and other resources. It would also provide for the transportation of intermediate-produced materials and goods. It would provide for the distribution of manufactured products as well. Besides overseeing all means of delivery for materials ranging from source items to finished products, the institution of transportation would ensure that all citizens have access to public means of travel.

The transportation institution would consist of a series of national conveyance and shipping centers with responsibility for land, water, and air travel. This institution would contain busing as well as trucking firms. It would contain authorities for subway and trolley car operations. It would contain monorail and railroad companies. Air transport and air passenger services would also be a part of the transportation institution. Ocean-based shipping companies and ferry services would be components as well. A center for transportation would build and maintain the public highways and thoroughfares. Similarly, another center would maintain the nation's railroad system. There would be a third transportation center that oversees the canals and waterways. Further, a fourth transportation center would build and operate the airports and maintain the accompanying airfields.

The universal institution of transportation will guarantee the distribution of food, clothing, and medicine throughout society. The transportation institution will ensure delivery of raw materials and supplies that are necessary to business and industry. It will also ensure the delivery of manufactured goods and products to the wholesalers and retailers. Further, the universal institution of transportation will provide for the transport of people as well. There will be public transportation available to all citizens who work in or are supported by the universal institution of employment.

Similar to the institution of communication, the universal institution of transportation will be governed by a managerial board comprised of executives chosen from participating transportation enterprises. The members to the managerial board will be elected to serve for designated periods of service.

In addition to the universal institution of transportation, there would be private enterprises operating across the transportation sector of society. These independently owned and operated companies would be established to meet the general shipping and transportation needs of society.

There should be established a universal institution of financial resource. This institution would be made up of major financial entities designed to serve the banking needs of society. It would offer savings, lending, and investment opportunities through banks and other financial houses. The universal financial institution would be utilized by all elements of society. This includes businesses and corporations that use funds to make capital improvements and expand their product line. It includes self-employed people who use available resources to enhance their economic situation. It includes individuals employed in the universal institution of employment, who secure funds to supplement their work benefits and amenities. It also includes citizens employed solely in the private sector of society, who wish to participate in the financial institution in order to secure funds to help meet living expenses This institution would contain accountants, bankers, financiers, financial planners, investors, investment managers, insurance adjusters, tax preparers, etc.

A major unit would be dedicated to personal banking and finance. It would meet all the banking needs of individual people. It will offer personal loans, education loans, auto loans, home improvement loans, etc. This unit will provide savings options including regular savings, certificates of deposit, and money market accounts. It will further offer checking account options for the citizenry of society.

Another unit would focus on the economic well-being of business. It would have banking sectors for self-employed individuals, small businesses, and large corporations. Various checking account options including basic, analyzed, and choice checking, which are geared to managing a business's financial needs, will be offered. It will offer commercial loans, short- and long-term loans, lines of credit, etc. This unit will also provide for construction and renovation loans. Business-based savings accounts, certificates of deposit, and money market accounts will be offered as well. Other financial support will include services for record management, payroll, tax withholding, health care coverage, and retirement management.

A third unit would be responsible for mortgages. Residential mortgage for primary housing will be a key service. Housing mortgages will also be provided for non-primary residences such as vacation homes, etc. Similarly, this unit will offer investment opportunities for rentable properties such as two-family dwellings, apartment buildings, and so forth. This unit will also offer refinancing options including second mortgages, home equity lines of credit, and reverse mortgages. For corporations, it will offer a line of commercial mortgages. In addition, it will offer inventory financing as well as various options on real estate financing.

A fourth unit would consist of insurance companies that provide an assortment of insurance packages. This unit will offer disability, health care, and extended health care coverage. It will offer dental insurance as well. It will also provide whole life, term life, and survivor benefit insurance policies. This unit will further offer home owner insurance, disaster (fire and flood) insurance, automobile insurance, etc. Insurances available to the business world would focus on job-related injury, workman's compensation, and workman's disability. Other business insurance options include coverage for liability, theft, and property damage.

A fifth unit would be comprised of companies offering investment opportunities to individuals and organizations alike. The investment firms would administer programs which give clients the opportunity to buy and sell stock, purchase bonds, purchase money market certificates, etc. As illustrated by investment options currently available in the United States, the companies will manage retirement investment accounts such as individual retirement accounts (IRAs), Roth accounts, and 401(k) plans. Other investment products will include saving bonds and college educational investment programs like the 529 plans. The investment unit will also provide an assortment of trust funds including testamentary trusts as well as revocable and irrevocable living trusts. For businesses, the investment companies will also manage various employee benefit, pension, and profit sharing accounts. Included will be health insurance, group life insurance, retirement 401 (k) plans, and company bonuses.

A sixth unit would consist of credit card companies. These companies would provide the means for individuals and businesses to purchase products and services on credit with predetermined payback schedules. Key responsibilities of this unit will be to maintain sound management of individual and corporate credit ratings, set appropriate limits on the amount of money that can be borrowed, carefully monitor interest rates, and determine reasonable payback schedules so credit card customers don't become burdened with excessively high debt.

A seventh unit would contain firms that provide support services to the financial sector of society. These include accounting firms, tax preparation services, financial planning offices, and investment advisory groups. Additional members include repossession firms and collection agencies.

Branch offices of each major unit within the institution of financial resource would operate in every community. There would be banks, mortgage companies, investment firms, and other financial entities put in place. The institution's units could be housed in the same building or they could reside as self-contained facilities. Besides the individual branch offices, citizens will have access to electronic banking via the internet as well as outlets for automated teller machines (ATMs). Corporations will have access to on-line business banking, clearing houses that automatically apply electronic credits and debits to corporate accounts, same-day wire transfers, and so on. Further, it's likely that many businesses and industries would have on-site satellite banking offices.

Similar to the institutions of communication and transportation, the universal institution of financial resource will be governed by a managerial board comprised of executives chosen from participating financial enterprises. The members to the managerial board will be elected to serve for designated periods of service.

In addition to the universal institution of financial resource, there would be private enterprises operating across the financial sector of society. These independently owned and operated banks, lending companies, investment firms, etc., would be established to meet the general finance and banking needs of society.

There should be established a universal institution of utility-service in society. The institution of utility-service would guarantee the operational and maintenance needs of society are met. It would make sure that drinking water is provided to all communities. Also, it would ensure that energy fuels such as heating oil and natural gas are supplied to the homes and businesses. It would ensure that power is supplied to the hospitals, schools, and housing projects. Similarly, it would ensure power is available to run the businesses and industries.

The institution of utility-service will ensure that electricity is available to all communities. That is, it will make sure the city streets have lighting. Also, it will be responsible for snow removal, thereby making sure the sidewalks and streets are plowed. It will make sure the garbage is collected and trash is removed. For all communities, it will ensure the treatment and disposal of sewage is taken care of. Likewise, the utility-service institution will ensure the storm sewers are in proper working order. The institution will make sure that city park lawns are mowed and public flower beds and shrubbery gardens are maintained. Overall, the universal institution of utility-service will ensure that all public facilities are operational and adequately staffed and serviced.

A key unit of the institution of utility-service would consist of a national fire department. Its function would be to respond to all structural fires within the community including fires involving homes, office buildings, shopping malls, etc. There will be fire stations built in every community and staffed with professional firefighters. The stations will be supplied with fire fighting equipment including water tanks, extinguishers, pumps, hoses, nozzles, and gauges. They will also be supplied with air tank compressors, plus breathing apparatus including air masks and respirators. They will also be supplied with rescue equipment including cutting tools such as saws and axes, rigging hardware including harnesses and carabiners, as well as extrication tools like pike poles and Halligan bars. The stations will house various models of fire trucks including fire engines and pumpers, water tenders and tank trucks, hook and ladder and tiller trucks, etc. The fire stations will also house emergency vehicles such as rescue trucks and ambulances.

The universal institution of utility-service will be governed by a managerial board comprised of executives chosen from participating utility enterprises. As with other major institutions of society, the members to the managerial board will be elected to serve for designated terms.

In addition to the universal institution of utility-service there would be private enterprises established throughout the utility field. The companies would be independently owned and operated, and they would function to help meet the daily operational and maintenance needs of society. Among the private enterprises would be independently run fire departments, volunteer fire departments, etc. Again, there would be no competition between the privately owned utility companies and those falling under the umbrella of the universal institution of utility-service.

There should be established a universal institution of energy that's comprised of a national network of energy suppliers and distributors. The energy institution would consist of hydroelectric plants, wind-power plants, electric companies, and oil companies. It would consist of coal plants, natural gas enterprises, solar energy providers, and nuclear power plants. The individuals employed as energy suppliers, i.e., the coal miners, oil well drillers, gas line contractors, and installers of oil and natural gas pipelines would belong to the institution of energy.

The national energy resources would be monitored through the institution of energy. Its role would be to oversee the generation, dissemination, and consumption of energy. Energy conservation would be the responsibility of this institution as well. So too would be designs for the establishment of long-term energy supplies, including plans for the development of new sources of energy. This institution will guarantee that supplies of energy are available to all sectors of society; that is, it will ensure the industrial, commercial, and residential components of society are afforded the energy resources they need. Additionally, the energy institution would work closely with the institution of utilities-services to ensure power is delivered to all appropriate outlets of society.

The universal institution of energy will be governed by a managerial board comprised of executives chosen from participating energy enterprises. Members to the managerial board will be elected to serve for designated terms.

Besides the universal institution of energy there would be private enterprises established throughout the fields of power and energy. These companies would be independently owned and operated. As with other major institutions of society, the private companies would function on their own to help meet the energy needs of people in society.

A universal institution of ecology should be established with the role of maintaining stability to the world's various eco-systems. One of its main responsibilities would be to monitor the quality of human life as it exists on Earth. The ecological institution would work to remove the poisons and toxins that are harmful to human health. To accomplish this, it would investigate the causes of contamination and pollution prevalent in urban areas and work to provide clean air and pure water to the cities, towns, and villages. It would also attempt to eliminate overcrowding as it pertains to poor housing conditions, inadequate food supplies, and sub-standard utility services. Thereby, it would help correct unsanitary living conditions which have high potential for the spread of disease. The institution of ecology will strive to make the world of man as safe as possible and ensure that the human species doesn't harm the environment in any way.

The institution of ecology would monitor the state of the environment as well. The ecology institution will work to prevent erosion and promote the development of fertile soil throughout the land. Additionally, it will work to improve purity of water in the streams, rivers, lakes, and seas. It will also address problems associated with air quality and strive to control and reduce airborne pollutants such as ozone and smog. Its overall objective then would be to stabilize and expand healthy eco-systems wherever they exist in the world.

Accordingly, the ecology institution will investigate the interactions between living organisms and their environment. It will study the life balances occurring in Nature, and assess the degree of competition and cooperation taking place among various species of life. It will study interactions of organisms with their environment, including the way gases like oxygen and carbon dioxide are exchanged, and the manner in which nitrogen is made available and utilized by plants and animals alike. It will also evaluate the ways in which minerals are exchanged between the living and nonliving worlds. Additionally, it will keep track of how water is utilized by living organisms. Further, it will document how animate life returns to Nature and then is used to revitalize the soil.

Finally, the institution of ecology would establish national agencies to promote the welfare of specie life in both the plant and animal kingdoms. It would establish environmentally-secure parks, forests, and wetlands. It would also expand natural wildlife and refuge areas. It would further strive to maintain a clean water environment for the oceans, seas, lakes, rivers, and streams. Overall, the ecological institution will work to improve the quality of life throughout Nature.

There should be established a universal institution on the environment proper. The institution of environment would focus on maintaining the stability of the inanimate components of the universe. This would include the earth with its tri-component lithosphere, hydrosphere, and atmosphere. Hence, it would involve rock structures, i.e., the boulders, shale, magma, and sedimentary rock. It would cover clay, sand, and soil as well. It would involve the aqua portion of the planet and include the oceans, seas, lakes, rivers, and streams. It would likewise take in all gases which comprise the atmosphere. A key charge of this institution would be to ensure that minerals, fossil fuels, and other natural resources are utilized in a safe and prudent manner.

This institution would function to make the environment as sound and safe possible. It will be involved with the study of earthquakes and volcanic activity. It will also participate in the study of tsunamis, floods, and freshets. Likewise, it will investigate the cause and effect of hurricanes, tornados, windstorms, and sandstorms. Along with the institution of ecology, the environmental institution will work to prevent erosion of the soil by wind and water. The two institutions will also work to preserve fresh water and clean air across all regions of the world. Additionally, the institution will be involved in efforts to sustain the blanketing effect of the atmosphere, which moderates surface temperature and shields the planet from excessive cosmic radiation. The overall goal of this institution then is to stabilize the environment and provide a safe haven for all creatures of life.

There should be established a universal institution of discovery. It would consist of a nation-wide association of research organizations dedicated to study of the natural and social sciences. The discovery institution would contain laboratories that focus on the fields of biology, chemistry, physics, and earth science. It would also involve research in the areas of astronomy, geology, and space exploration. It would involve studies in the areas of chemical, mechanical, electrical, and civil engineering. Likewise, the discovery institution would contain research centers dedicated to the study of agriculture, botany, and animal life. The discovery institution would contain research facilities dedicated to the study of the human body including the subjects of health care, medicine, nutrition, etc. This institution would house investigative labs which focus on the study of human behavior as well. Basically, the institution of discovery would promote scientific study in all areas of human endeavor.

The institution of discovery would focus on new inventions and processes, and accordingly, promote the infusion of the latest technologies across society. Whether acquired from land-based experiments, studies conducted under the sea, or investigations performed via space exploration, the new technologies would be part of the discovery institution.

The institution of discovery will collect information from all established places of learning. It will compile and distribute data whether derived from research conducted at business and commercial locations or industrial and manufacturing sites. It will collect and disseminate new knowledge whether derived from schools and universities or medical facilities and hospitals. The institution would further ensure advancements that are made through research and development are secured. To do this, the institution would establish libraries and museums to preserve the improvements gleaned through discovery.

As with the other major institutions of society, the institutions of ecology, environment, and discovery will be governed by managerial boards that are comprised of executives chosen from their respective participating enterprises. Again, the members to the managerial boards of these institutions will be elected to serve for specified terms.

In addition, there would be private enterprises established throughout the fields of ecology, environment, and discovery. The companies would be independently owned and operated. The private ecological companies would function to help maintain sound ecological management of the particular ecosystems they're involved with. Private companies within the environmental arena would function to sustain secure habitats for the world's living community. And private companies associated with discovery and invention would function to meet the technological and informational needs across society. Reflective of the other institutions, there wouldn't be competition between the privately owned companies and the public enterprises associated with the universal institutions of ecology, environment, and discovery.

It's important to recognize that private sector businesses and industries will account for a significant portion of the enterprises that populate the world's social-economic systems. Indeed, all areas of human endeavor, including those represented by a universal institution, will have a high percentage of businesses and industries residing in the private sector. As noted before, all businesses and industries associated with the universal institutions of society will focus on the fundamental needs of mankind. The private sector businesses and industries not associated with universal institutions will also serve the basic needs of mankind, such that they're in place mainly for the citizens who will neither require nor depend upon the public sector counterparts.

To be sure, the private sector enterprises are necessary and central to the large number of people who will seek employment in both the public and private sector realms. We've already discussed areas of societal life where the crossover businesses and industries are located. As noted, they are in the areas of housing, clothing, and food acquisition. They're in the areas of education, health care, and recreation. And they're in the areas of communication, transportation, utilities-services, energy, etc.

We should further point out there're a number of areas of social living that are represented by private sector enterprises only. In fact, most of the non-basic needs of mankind will be handled through the private sector. Some of the non-essential amenities and conveniences we're referring to include the products and services associated with the home and garden businesses. They also include specialty products from the jewelry business, arts and crafts stores, etc. They include the sales from party supply and toys stores. They also include outlets associated with stationary supplies, flower shops, and pet stores. They include the services of lawn care specialists, home decor representatives, and real estate and travel agents. Other endeavors which fall within the private sector include the operation of gift shops, beauty shops and barber shops.

In regard to the housing industry, homes and apartment buildings reside in both the public and private sectors. The hotel and motel businesses however would be located solely within the private sector. Relative to the food industry, the public sector will have cafeterias and dining facilities set aside for people to meet their needs of subsistence. Nonetheless, the restaurant business in general would reside in the private sector. Along with the assortment of cuisine-based restaurants such as Chinese, Italian, French, American, etc. the private sector would contain the donut shops, pizza shops, ice cream parlors, and so forth. Throughout society, both public and private enterprises would complement one another as they function to meet the overall needs of the citizens.

9

Evolution of Culture

THE MOST SIGNIFICANT DEVELOPMENT in the history of modern man has been the advances made in social living. As far as biological evolution is concerned, the human species hasn't experienced any notable adjustments during the last 1,500 to 2,000 generations of births. From a cultural standpoint, however, the human race has progressed considerably.

Human culture has evolved. In recent times, mankind has expanded and refined the two major institutions of religion and government. Man has also introduced and developed the vast social and economic systems we live under today. Overall, the human species has transformed its pattern of living from an isolated, cave dwelling existence to a socially orientated, urban-based lifestyle.

Over the past several thousand years, the species of man has changed its lifestyle tremendously. At one time, walking was the only means of travel. But now man enjoys a number of motorized means of transportation for he assembles automobiles, buses, and trains to move him about on land. He constructs boats, ships, and ocean liners to carry him over the seas as well as submarines to take him underwater. Similarly, man builds hot air balloons, helicopters, and airplanes to carry him into the sky. Furthermore, he designs and builds rocket ships which are capable of transporting him to new locations across the solar system.

From living in tents, lean-tos, and caves, cultural evolution has progressed to where man resides in an assortment of well-designed homes made of lumber and brick. He builds houses which are styled as ranches, split-levels, colonials, and so forth. He builds fancy restaurants to dine in, and elaborate hotels and motels to stay in. He designs high-rise apartment complexes and sprawling housing tracts in which to live. Indeed, cultural evolution has enabled man to construct extravagant structures made of concrete and steel. For example, he builds bowling alleys, indoor golf ranges, and gigantic sport stadiums in which to play and compete. He builds huge shopping malls to shop in, and giant convention centers to gather and meet in. He builds banks, libraries, and museums as well. He constructs magnificent office buildings and towering skyscrapers in which to conduct his business. He builds multi-building factories and industrial parks to serve as manufacturing sites for the many household products he uses on a daily basis.

From working with hand carved bone and stone utensils, man's cultural development has resulted in the use of numerous, intricately-designed instruments and tools. In today's world, man assembles electrical tools like the electric screwdriver, drill, and sander. He assembles power tools like the stapler, nail gun, grinder, planer, and electric saw. He designs electrical motors and gas powered engines. He puts together instruments which include the wrist watch, microphone, and hearing aid. He produces printers, copiers, and fax machines. He assembles computers and cell phones. He also fabricates an assortment of household appliances including the toaster, microwave oven, dishwasher, clothes washer, etc. Man builds equipment for communication including the telegraph, telephone, radio, and television. He builds vehicles for transportation that include the bicycle, automobile, train, boat, and airplane. He constructs farm equipment such as the tractor, cultivator, and combine. He also designs and installs machinery in factories which allow him to forge parts and then assemble the parts into an assortment of useful products.

Throughout history, mankind has made major advances in the field of medicine. He discovers vaccines to protect himself from the diseases of small pox, tuberculosis, and polio. He develops serums with antibodies and antitoxins that are designed to combat and destroy harmful bacteria and viruses. He produces antihistamines to ease the discomforts of allergies, and he manufactures cold tablets to counteract the symptoms of the common cold. He synthesizes birth control pills to prevent pregnancy, and he develops vascular enhancement drugs to treat the problem of erectile dysfunction.

Over the centuries man has developed the fine arts of theater, dance, and music. Man's achievements in fine arts are represented by the following artistic compositions. He paints notable works of art like Da Vinci's *Mona Lisa* and Gainsborough's *The Blue Boy*. He sculptures magnificent statues like Rodin's *The Thinker* and Michelangelo's *Pieta*. He writes and performs superb operas including Mozart's *Don Giovanni* and Wagner's *Lohengrin*. He writes great symphonies including Beethoven's *Symphony Number 9* and Schubert's *Unfinished Symphony*. He presents superb musical performances like *The Sound of Music* and *Man of La Mancha*. He produces enjoyable motion pictures like *Gone with the Wind* and *Casablanca*. Further, he writes outstanding novels including Pasternak's *Dr. Zhivago* and Steinbeck's *The Grapes of Wrath*.

Man has developed major religions which instruct people on ways to venerate an omnipresent, omnificent, and omnipotent being. The religions of the world offer people the opportunity to focus on spiritual awareness, as well as provide them with a template for sound moral guidance. Through a deep devotion to religious doctrine, man is called upon to install elaborate worship services and rituals. Similarly, the devotion to religious doctrine inspires man to build ornate and beautiful mosques, temples, and cathedrals.

Man has instituted governments characterized by varying degrees of citizen participation in the decision-making process. The role of the world's governments is to bring about social order and maintain behavioral standards common to everyone. They also attempt to apply equitable consequences for the acts of misbehavior. Man establishes systems of government which are democratic, monarchal, and totalitarian in operational and structural design.

Man has developed socio-economic systems based on differing means to control the distribution of goods and services. He formulates economic systems which focus on the operating principles of capitalism, free enterprise, collectivism, socialism, etc. These systems influence the extent of economic opportunity that's available to the citizens, as well as determine the distribution of wealth across all sectors of society.

The cultural evolution which has occurred to date has been extensive. We're well aware of the wide range of ceremonial activities that are part of the world of man. Among them are the following. Man circumcises the baby boy, and he practices sterilization as a means of birth control. He institutes ceremonies to mark the occurrence of birthdays and anniversaries as well as the ascension of young people into adulthood. Likewise, he acknowledges their graduation from high school and college. Another significant ceremonial activity is the celebration of the union of a husband and wife through marriage. Additionally, man institutes recognition parties for co-workers as they complete their careers and retire. For organizations, man holds award ceremonies to acknowledge significant accomplishments such as reaching a milestone in the productivity goals of a business, or attaining the monetary goal of a charitable group. Further, he holds banquets to recognize feats of athleticism which signify success in the sports' world. Finally, man constructs symbolic markers to honor the dead. These markers range from small white crosses, like those lining the cemeteries of Arlington, Virginia, to the elaborate pyramids sprinkled along the Nile valley of Egypt. All of the rites and rituals mankind now practices represent the tremendous expansion of human culture over the past several-hundred, thousand years.

It took centuries for the present day social-economic systems to come to fruition. Over time, great civilizations were built up and then destroyed. From a historical perspective, some of the civilizations were short in duration and of little consequence. Others were longer lasting and significant. The significant ones had a strong influence on the cultural development of man. They advanced the principles of law and order and laid the foundation for what's universally accepted as proper social behavior.

Early on, the cultural development of man moved forward at a slow and steady pace. In recent times, however, it has proceeded in explosive fashion. Through it all, man's social world became more complex as various components of society became highly specialized. As society progressed, the manufacture of goods and products became more reliable and the services performed by citizens proved to be more varied and useful. Over the past few centuries, the benefits afforded through social living have expanded to unforeseen heights.

Human culture proceeds with the acquisition of new knowledge derived from previous knowledge. It involves the application of new skills built on older skills. As we've pointed out, cultural evolution doesn't happen overnight, for major social advances take place over extended periods of time. Great discoveries and key accomplishments require considerable effort from a host of people working together during a significant portion of their careers. For example, the discovery of the cures of polio and tuberculosis involved years of tedious research by a large number of medical scientists. Similarly, the first manned flights to the moon only occurred after decades of rocket tests and space-simulation experiments conducted by thousands of flight technicians and aeronautical engineers.

Cultural heritage has mushroomed because man put his mind to work. As a creature of thought, he began to utilize his mental capabilities more effectively. He utilized his ability to think in the abstract, rationalize, and visualize the future. Above all, he utilized his ability to create. Man invented mathematics. He developed the sciences of physics, chemistry, biology, etc., and then applied the learning from these sciences to his everyday world.

The application of technology resulting from the natural sciences was highly beneficial to the advancement of human culture. Equally important was the development of the social sciences. Man has formulated religions. He's drawn up ecclesiastical doctrine and written moral code to which he ascribes. Man has likewise established governments. He's drafted laws and defined the basic concepts of right and wrong. Man also installed a social order to life. He established rules of behavior and applied them to his daily routine.

In examining the development of societal life, we should remember the human organism didn't spring up as an independent species of life. Rather, the human species arrived as a product of preexisting life and was born into an eco-system that was well established. As with other creatures of life, man began to affect the environment when he appeared on the scene. In the early days, man was mostly a benefactor of the eco-system into which he was born. As cultural evolution proceeded, however, he became more of a contributor. He began to influence his environment in deliberate and less deliberate ways.

Man has come a long way in his ability to affect the environment. With bulldozers he's able to carve down plateaus and mountains. He's also able to build up marshlands with fill of rock, gravel, and topsoil. He can dig out river basins, construct dams, and cause new lakes to be formed. He can irrigate the desert in order to allow life to flourish. Man can cut down trees to clear land for farming and provide lumber for housing. He can grade flatlands and then blacktop the flatlands to create parking lots for automobiles. He can mine coal and burn it to produce heat and energy. And he can drill for oil. He can refine gasoline and use it as fuel for his cars. To improve water quality, he can stock ponds and lakes with marine life that consume undesirable algae. Using pesticides, he can spray and destroy blight-causing organisms which bring disease to plant life. In physical, chemical, and biological ways, man can add value to his ecosystem. In a like manner, he can do it harm.

Man can shape his immediate environment. However, he cannot alter major events taking place in the world at large. For example, man cannot stop an earthquake from happening, prevent a volcano from erupting, nor shut down the high winds of a tornado. Neither can he stop the earth from spinning on its axis, nor reverse the direction it takes as it travels around the sun.

Nevertheless, man can exert a measured amount of influence on his ecosystem. As we described, he can landscape the environment. Under proper atmospheric conditions, he can make it rain if he wants to. He can also redirect a waterfall and use its new flow to irrigate arid lands. Furthermore, he can build a windmill to harness the wind and use it as a reliable source of energy.

Of more significance is the fact that man can make himself somewhat independent of the environment. In other words, he's able to free himself from various environmental restrictions. That is, he can construct homes to protect himself from the wind, rain, and snow. And he can utilize fossil fuels to heat those homes. He can also build reservoirs to collect drinking water and deliver it to his homes through elaborate piping systems. Additionally, man can prepare foods and preserve the foods through canning and freezing processes. Further, by means of roadways and railways, he can easily transport the food and other supplies to his communities and homes. Such capabilities make it possible for people to live anywhere on Earth regardless of immediate environmental conditions.

Given the technological advances made in social living, man is able to travel across the earth's surface irrespective of local environmental conditions. While on land he can travel by automobile, bus, or train. If secured within environmentally protective ships, man can travel above, on, or below the seas. For travel upon water, he can utilize barges, boats, and ocean vessels. Similarly, he can travel underwater in the submarines. For travel in the skies, man can fly in the pressurized cabins of airplanes or spaceships. He can travel in hot air balloons and helicopters as well. As attested to by submarine and spaceship travel, man's been able to encapsulate environmental conditions which are necessary for human existence. On a limited basis, he's been able to transport himself vis-a-vis these conditions to all regions of the planet.

Through a restructuring of the earth's terrain, man can create, destroy, or alter entire ecosystems. As he landscapes the earth's topography, he influences the development of life and affects the evolution of other species as well as his own. Over a period of time, man has become the custodian of numerous species of plant and animal life. This is demonstrated in different ways. For example, man breeds cattle at will and slaughters lambs to his gourmet's delight. He produces hybridized variations of grains and crops.

Likewise, he enhances the yield of fruit orchards and increases the output from vegetable gardens. Through genetic engineering, he even introduces new species of life. Mankind has domesticated some species of life and he's destroyed others. At various times, his activities have nearly wiped out certain species of animals such as the Alaskan seal, the bald eagle, and the North American buffalo.

Thus, man is an influential player as far as the ecological balance of the world is concerned. If he chooses, man can alter the environment to varying extents and thereby affect the quality of life. Because of this capability, mankind must be deliberate in what he does. That is, he must be careful not to harm stable ecosystems. It's man's responsibility to maintain a healthy environment wherever it exists and hence protect the development of animate life on Earth.

To be the guardian of the various species of life places man in a special role. It puts him in the position of being the provider and protector of animate life. Indeed, man's inherent benevolent nature obligates him to protect the environment and its inhabitants. The survival of the multitude of species depends upon how successful he is in maintaining and enriching the world's several ecosystems. To the best of his ability, he's obliged to provide the greatest good for the largest possible number of specie life.

As far as cultural development is concerned, the aspects of social life that need not change shouldn't be changed. Rather, they should be kept intact and preserved. Conversely, for the features that need improvement, man should attempt to improve.

As we look at man's place in the world, we might wonder if biological evolution forecasts the path cultural development takes. Indeed, there's a trend to the way the cultural world of man progressed which correlates to how biological evolution proceeded. We know within the biological world, today's organisms evolved from very primitive cells. Modern-day organisms are thousands of times more complex than their single-celled ancestors. Similar to the evolution of animate life, human culture mushroomed tremendously from its early Cro-Magnon beginnings. There's no question that biological evolution influences the cultural development of man. For sure, man's psychological capabilities are determined by the level of actualization of the human brain; and in many ways, cultural progress reflects the state of refinement of the mental facilities of man.

If the human gene pool eventually becomes totally homogenous, will this lead to cultural unity as well? That is, can a single species of organism called mankind develop a social structure common for all nations, or must man always be separated by cultural barriers as typified by the social diversities of language, ethnicity, economic status, politics, and religious beliefs?

We might ask if mankind should continue to be separated by non-biological barriers established through custom and tradition, or should the barriers be eliminated? Can a universal social-economic structure be put in place for people to live under? Is there a government design that will protect the rights of all? Likewise, can a common religion exist that everyone's willing to ascribe to? And is it possible to install a broad-based employment structure where jobs are provided with benefits guaranteed to everyone who's willing to work? There's one answer to these questions, and it is yes! There can be a universal social-economic structure, a single government, and one religion for everyone.

As a matter of fact, there ought to be universal institutions established across society to make it function more effectively. Society would be better organized and the needed services would be delivered in a more efficient manner. What's more, the establishment of universal institutions of government, religion, etc. would draw people together through common ties and shared goals. Furthermore, the universal institutions would provide additional opportunities which don't exist now in the areas of employment, education, health care, communication, transportation, and recreation.

Oddly enough, there are several institutions in existence today which can be classified as universal in nature. However, the classification is based on intent of operation and not on structure or functional design. For example, there is a "non-formalized" universal institution of government in the world. To a certain extent, the non-formalized universal institution is reflected in the design of the United Nations. However, the United Nations doesn't rule over the political interests of its individual members. In nearly all cases, member countries place their own interests above the agenda of the United Nations. Likewise, there's a non-formalized universal institution of religion in the world. Most of the time, however, the world's major religions put their individual doctrine and hierarchies above it. Also, there is a non-formalized universal institution of education in the world. However, in most cases the nations place secular interests above the need to maintain equitable worldwide educational standards. Such "non-formalized" institutions reside across the several societies of mankind in varying degrees of sophistication.

The extent to which the "non-formalized" institutions are universal and in place today, is derived from social behavior in its theoretical sense. For government, the universality comes about because of a worldwide desire for freedom, equality, and justice under the law. For religion, the universality comes about based on a belief in the divine, the quest for a moral compass, and an acceptance of the basic goodness of mankind. For education, the universality occurs due to a desire to provide the necessary level of training for young people so they can achieve an adequate standard of living via successful employment.

Someday, the commonalities of theoretical principles will transform into practical accords of conduct. Someday, the non-formalized design of these institutions will be replaced with systems which are much more definitive. And someday, the universality nature of these institutions will be sanctioned on a worldwide basis.

We've already seen that human beings behave the same regardless of the social structure they live under. We know, for example, that people in every society educate their young. Everywhere, people build homes and seek ways to be safe from the elements. All people seek medical attention in order to maintain their health. Likewise, people everywhere establish a police force and legal system to protect themselves from the criminal elements of society. People the world over follow the religion which gives them spiritual strength and moral guidance.

The values that people hold dear are standard throughout the world and cut through racial, ethnical, and tribal barriers. As we know, all human beings believe in justice and hold common standards as to what is right or wrong. Most people, for example, know that it's wrong to harm another person in either physical or emotional ways. Nearly everyone believes it's wrong to lie, cheat, and steal. Children everywhere know they should respect and honor their parents and grandparents. Further, all people know they should love their family and care for others on a humanitarian level.

People the world over behave the same even though their religious views conflict at times. People the world over live the same even though their governments often oppose each other. Basically, all human beings follow the same daily living patterns even though their social-economic systems vary substantially. The day will come when basic human values, as we've described, become key factors in the design of societal institutions. When that happens, the people of the world will be united as one.

In the long run, the world's societies must subordinate their interests to the concerns of a universal society of man. On matters of ending hostilities and maintaining truces, the governments of the United States and Russia, as well as all other nations, must work in unison to promote peace on a worldwide basis. Indeed, national governments must support the decisions of a fair and just world-governing body first, and themselves second, on issues which promote stability and peace throughout the world. In the area of religion, the Protestants and the Catholics must represent the Christian faith first and themselves second. Additionally, the religions of Islamism, Taoism, Judaism, Christianity, Hinduism, and Confucianism must not let ritual or ceremonial differences overshadow a common commitment to enhance the spiritual life of man. Eventually, the people of the world will be united. Eventually, the cultural evolution of man will lead to one universal government, a universal religion, and a universal social-economic system. Eventually, a single social structure will emerge to encompass all sectors of humanity.

Someday there will be established a "United Nations" type government comprised of representatives from the various world governments. Likewise, there will be established a "United Nations" type religious entity comprised of representatives from the several world religions. Someday there will be a "United Nations" type employment organization comprised of members from major world employers, or representatives from specific job categories such as farmer, factory worker, restaurant worker, software engineer, lawyer, etc. Someday there will be separate "United Nations" type organizations which represent the other major components of societal living including education, health care, transportation, communication, energy, recreation, etc. All the individual components of these universal institutions will become members because they want to. The various national governments, independent religions, etc., will join their respective world body association on a voluntary basis.

When a single social structure does emerge, it'll be one where a person is able to earn a living and pursue his purpose in life. The universal society will be one in which every individual is able to contribute his time and resources toward the betterment of mankind. The institutions will be structured to help each person meet his physiological needs of survival as well as his psychological needs of personal fulfillment. The institutions will be structured so education and health care are guaranteed to everyone who is willing to work. A person will be able to pursue a career in which he's interested; and in that chosen career, he'll be successful to the extent his skills and abilities allow. The universal social structure then will be one that's best suited for the majority of people in the world.

What should the various nations of the world do in regard to the pursuit of a universal culture of man? We note that diversity among the people of the world exists because of different customs and beliefs. Diversified cultures result in economic differences, employment disparities, and varying standards of living. We further note that differences in governments and religions, for example, occur because people want it that way. The people of the world desire to maintain their tribal, ethnical, racial, and sub-racial identities. Regardless of historical background, however, it's the responsibility of the nations of the world to direct human culture so it advances the positive accomplishments of social living.

What should individual people do in regard to the pursuit of a universal culture? On an individual basis, everyone should realize he's biologically and psychologically identical to all other members of his species. None of the dividing forces we refer to are the product of biological evolution. The only basis for people not to be equal lies in the route taken by human culture. It's the individual's responsibility to help shape society's future state by respecting the differences of other people and trying to implement improvements based on the similarities they display.

Someday there will be a single culture of man. There will be only one language and one nationality. There will be only one government, and no doubt, one religion. It is known that other species of life evolve into a homogeneous group; and for the most part, it's been necessary for their survival. A species which ends up in a homogeneous group lives longer than a species that remains in several isolated groups. The adaptability for the homogeneous group is greater than it is for any of the individual (separate) collections of organisms. In all probability, the species of man will follow the same route taken by other species of life. Eventually, mankind will become a homogeneous unit with one social structure. And as a matter of practicality, why shouldn't he? Why shouldn't mankind persist in the world as a dynamic, unified species of animate life?

Thus far, man has brought down the physical barriers that have kept his species divided. Now he must eliminate the nonphysical barriers, i.e., the cultural divisions that keep him separated. Man can do this in one of two ways. He can do it through a prohibitive, negative approach. That is, he could do it by social programming, intimidation, or conquest. Alternatively, he can do it in a constructive manner. He could accomplish it through acceptance and mutual respect for one another. The constructive approach would require communication, cooperation, and the sharing of success. If there's any question as to which way to proceed, obviously, the only acceptable way is for the people of the world to cooperate and work together to achieve social progress.

The human species must unite and function as a single force for the purpose of improving society. People everywhere must continue to make contributions that advance the quality of life. Indeed, people have nothing better to do with their lives. Likewise, they have nothing better to do with their time. To make the improvements needed, people must revise the priorities of their personal lives and then evaluate and reestablish the priorities of society as a whole.

Can the people of the world meet together and discuss the type of society they want? Of course they can! Over the years, they have already done this in various social, economical, and political forums. Isn't it true that nearly everyone wants peace in the world? Isn't it true that everyone wants personal freedom, and doesn't everyone desire law and order in society? Doesn't every person want to be able to secure good health care and have the opportunity to an education? Doesn't every person want to pursue meaningful employment in the workplace with an equal chance to succeed? The people of the world can plan and work together to resolve their differences. They can find a common, standard basis for the positive resolution of the issues raised by these questions.

How does mankind put in place the social-economic structure we've outlined? One way the newly designed social-economic system could be implemented is given below.

It could begin on a small scale at first. Initially, there would be a group of dedicated individuals and enterprises brought together. The program could begin within a single community with just one factory or place of business involved. It could begin in a single school district with just one learning center involved. It could begin within a single health care network with just one hospital included. To administer the program, a governing board comprised of participating members would be set up.

The new social-economic system would start out in an experimental stage. As it became more successful, it would expand. Little by little, it would grow and expand to encompass other industries, other learning centers, and other medical facilities. With time and proven success, it would advance from one community to another.

Over a period of time, perhaps several decades, people would be in a position to establish the universal institutions we've described. Thus, a redesigned social-economic system might encompass a lone province or state at first. It could then expand to take in a single country. With time, it could spread across a continent to encompass several nations. If successful, it would eventually spread throughout the world. It's important to point out the establishment of a universal social-economic system would proceed at a pace the social, economical, and political conditions allow. Further, it would proceed in a democratically decided and peaceful manner.

The function of the universal institutions of employment, education, health care, and so forth, is not to replace the private sectors of society. The role is not to discourage the operation of private schools, nonpublic hospitals, independently owned businesses and industries, etc. The role of a universal social-economic system is not to restrict the free enterprise or capitalistic design of economic management. Neither is the role of the universal institutions to interfere with the conduct of societal programs of subsistence relief. For instance, it would not compete with charitable organizations that function satisfactorily in the private sector of society.

It's important to note that the participants in the public institutions which include employees, businesses, corporations, and so forth, will not be afforded any advantages over the participants within the private sector of society. Taxation and regulations, benefits and amenities, opportunities and entitlements, will be balanced equally between the private and public sectors of society. Proportionally based, the members of the public sector will contribute at the same level of employment and financial support as will the participants of the private sector.

The role of the universal social-economic system then is to provide a major avenue for successful social living. Its role is to give everyone a chance for good health care, a sound education, and a meaningful job. The role of the universal social-economic system is to upgrade the people's standard of living on a worldwide basis. In addition, it will give everyone the opportunity to identify with a worthwhile and constructive cause, and the chance to promote the positive accomplishments of mankind. The universal social-economic system offers tremendous potential for success and the people of the world ought to get to it.

Certainly a universal social-economic system can one day come about. Important to understanding how it will come about is the realization that the entire social-economic system is decided by man. Cultural evolution develops the way people want it to develop. Man possesses the free will to plan for and determine his future. Thereby, he's free to evolve the type of social-economic system he desires.

Mankind has freedom of choice. He is free to believe in a supreme being and a life hereafter. He is free to study Nature and learn about the world.

Also, he's free to work in an occupation of his choice. He is free to secure food and clothing, and he's free to build a home in which to live. Also, he is free to seek pleasure and happiness in life. Further, man is free to live in peace and develop the type of society he wants.

If man is free to evolve his society and free to live in peace, then why doesn't he live in peace now? Why hasn't world peace been attained to date; and if it requires evolution, how much longer will it take?

World peace is one of the major goals mankind has always desired. The end to one nation waging war against another has been sought since the beginning of human history. Relatively speaking, at the close of World War II, there was good opportunity for world peace. The world's major nations had just emerged from a devastating conflict and the futility demonstrated in the destruction of property and loss of human life was widely recognized. However, world peace didn't materialize and new wars broke out in Korea and Vietnam. Once again, the citizens of the world recognized the wastefulness of war and the destruction of life and limb that it causes. Truces were drawn up once more. But to the dismay of mankind, the quest for world peace still hasn't reached a satisfactory conclusion.

Additionally, it's been demonstrated that wars can be domesticated at times, for during major conflicts, cease-fires are requested and generally respected. Typically, this takes place on declared holy days. It was true, for instance, during the Vietnam conflict. Even thousands of years before, truces were respected at designated times. Such was the case with the conduct of the Olympic Games in ancient Greece, for back then, warring city-states ceased their hostilities every four years. For weeks at a time, the city-states afforded safe passage to both competitors and spectators so they could travel freely to and from the site of the games.

The humane treatment of captured adversaries is another war-related consideration that's valued by nations of the world. In 1949, the Geneva Convention adopted policies regarding the fair and compassionate treatment of prisoners of war. The policies adopted in Geneva, Switzerland, remain acceptable to most nations regardless of how bitter the rivalries become.

If people everywhere understand the futility of maiming and killing one another during battle, and if they agree to pre-declared truces which are honored in the midst of hostilities, then why can't nations eliminate war altogether? Why can't mankind solve the seemingly solvable problems pertaining to war and peace? Is the goal too difficult to achieve? Or, is the desire to intimidate and dominate other nations too strong to overcome?

It appears the reason why world peace hasn't been attained to date has nothing to do with man's ability to achieve it. Rather, it's due to a misplacement of values. Today, people don't want world peace, or they have little desire to achieve it. People know that certain goals such as world peace are within reach, and the nations of the world can lay down their arms if they really want to. Indeed, they can avoid hostilities and put an end to the bloodshed.

If mankind can actually attain a number of goals in life, then why doesn't he? Could the reason be that man wonders what lies beyond? Does he ask what goals are left if a number of goals lie, or appear to lie, within reach? Perhaps the dilemma the nations of the world and individual people face is that a void will occur when a goal is attained. A human being must always look ahead to the next higher goal, and if none exists, what happens then? If that's the case, then it appears in order to be happy, a man must constantly be striving towards a goal.

Must man always strive towards a goal but never achieve it completely? Is that a characteristic of the human station in life? Is it a reflection of the persistence of the human spirit? Is a human being a creature who derives as much pleasure, if not more, out of striving for a goal rather than attaining it? In other words, does a person enjoy building a castle as much or even more than he enjoys living in it?

In recent times, mankind has made significant progress in some key fields of endeavor. Several major goals of the human race have been realized. What were once unattainable dreams have now become everyday realities. One example is man's ability to harness and utilize electricity, a phenomenon of Nature that was highly feared at one time. Man has been able to generate electricity and use it to light his homes and power his businesses. Man also has been able to takes advantage of the natural resources which exist around him. For hundreds of thousands of years they lay unnoticed, underground; but today, he "mines" those resources to produce energy. He heats his homes and factories with the coal, oil, and natural gas extracted from the earth's crust. Further, man is able to refine crude oil to produce gasoline, a fuel which powers his automobiles and trucks. Another example of a fulfilled dream is the ability of man to take to the air. Through the use of airplanes and helicopters man flies in the sky, a feat that was once reserved to birds alone. Another unforeseen accomplishment has to do with the advances made in the state of human health. For example, in modern western societies like America, the life expectancy has nearly doubled during the past two hundred years. Thus far, man has found ways to basically eliminate the major diseases of tuberculosis, smallpox, polio, and so forth.

Although there are a number of goals which have been realized, there are other goals like an end to crime and the attainment of world peace that haven't. That is to say, mankind hasn't yet achieved all there is to achieve. The species of man needs renewed vision if it wishes to put an end to crime or secure world peace. The human species then needs to elevate its motivational drive to the next level to accomplish the hitherto unaccomplished goals.

Today, the citizens of the world have more time to address the problems and concerns that confront them. They don't need to work twelve to sixteen hours a day just to meet their basic needs of survival. Also, they live longer. They have more time to pursue scientific inquiry through investigative study and experimentation. They have more time to think about philosophical issues as well. People have more time to search for an "idealistic" world order.

Thus far, man has succeeded in the utilization of knowledge. He's been able to apply knowledge to improve life's conditions both at home and at work. In addition, the level of education has advanced for every demographic group of society. Children are better educated. Adults receive better training on the job and are afforded a greater opportunity to succeed in the workplace. With the continued dissemination of information, the people of the world are better prepared to carry on the vigorous efforts needed to improve social living.

Overall, society has become considerably more efficient at producing basic goods and delivering needed services. This has left more time for people to pursue new interests in life.

Human culture continues to evolve. Throughout the years, there have been a number of changes regarding the way people live. As discussed, there's been a major alteration to the world's employment structure. The occupations of today are highly specialized and much more technical than in the past. There has been realignment of the educational systems as well. The trend has been towards more broad-based, public educational designs. Likewise, there has been change in the pursuits of leisure time activities. New forms of entertainment have come into existence, many of which are mechanically-founded like auto racing, or electronically-based such as video and computer games. In addition, there's been a significant change to the way people utilize mobility throughout society, with many more communication and transportation avenues open to them. People communicate via social media and the Internet to share information on a host of topics. Because people are mobile and can easily pull up stakes, they have greater access to new jobs and different places to live. Even the benefits derived via the health care industry have changed. Due to better nutrition and improved medicines, people live longer and healthier lives. Finally, the attitudes in regard to family life have changed measurably as people are more tolerant of varying life styles. For instance, in many societies there's greater acceptance of premarital sex, abortion, homosexuality, and divorce.

The changing social values have an effect upon the way people view their role in life. However, changes in social values don't necessarily mean people are more secure or satisfied. Much of a person's peace of mind depends upon what his values are and where they're taking him. As we might expect, not everyone has been able to attain a sense of intrinsic worth. Likewise, not everyone's been able to acquire spiritual awareness through his or her religion. Consequently, there are people who turn to visions which lead nowhere or in the wrong direction. That's to say, many people turn to various cults, unorthodox ideologies, and even psychedelic drugs in an attempt to find a focus in life.

There is one aspect of human character that hasn't changed with time however. That aspect is, human beings still want a cause to live by. People have always wanted a cause to live by. And to get to where mankind feels he's pursuing the right cause, he must reassess his value system. As stated earlier, man must reset priorities and strive to improve his moral and spiritual commitment to social living. The human race has to restructure society and its several institutions. Society ought to be designed so the institutions instill in man the desire to pursue and attain his purpose in life.

We know that the human being is a creature of action. He wants to do something extra in life and something important. To find the means to accomplish this, mankind needs support and direction. The "place" where he finds support and direction is with God. Indeed, man must look to GOD for guidance, and with God's help, man will go where destiny takes him.

10

Perspective

There's a similarity between human beings and members of the animal kingdom as it pertains to the way they conduct their daily lives. In chapter 5, we noted that the institution of government was derived from the natural government of man. We said that every organism has its own natural government, which represents the way it inherently responds to events in life. If we look at various species of higher developed animals, we see they instinctively behave in ways that are reflective of how human beings behave. For sure, members of the animal community have similar behavioral patterns when it comes to family, government, education, health care, and so forth. As far as the institution of family is concerned, we can see correlations between mankind and other animals. For example, we see it in a mother robin as she scours the garden to finds worms to feed her newborn. We see the importance of family in a group of water buffalo who fend off a pack of hyenas trying to capture a vulnerable member of the herd. When we talk about the institution of education, we can see it in the actions of a mother lion as she teaches her offspring the skill of chasing down a zebra. Likewise, we see education in a mother bear as she teaches her cubs to snatch the salmon that are scaling the rapids. As far as health care is concerned, a housecat that's been involved in a fight with another animal finds its way home to lick its wounds. And so it goes!

We're aware then every species of organism behaves in a certain way relative to its biological and psychological makeup. And when we talk about family, we see it's an important facet of an animal's life and the organism responds accordingly. This is also true of other significant aspects of social behavior which people and animals engage in.

At this point, it's worthwhile to identify the origins of the desire to secure a more satisfying way of life through our social institutions. When we consider the place of religion in human affairs, we recognize there's a basic level of spirituality associated with every human being. It's a part of our inherent nature to express awe in the meaning and value of life. It's likewise a part of our nature to express appreciation for the one who created it. Hence, the sense of spirituality is present in man. Religion was given directly to man by God via creation of man's innate nature. Similarly, family, government, education, and health care are also based on man's fundamental character. Derived from God, our innate nature is determined by the biological composition of the body and how it's designed to function, specifically in the way the brain is supposed to perform. Indeed, our quest for family, religion (spirituality), government, education, health care, etc., are instinctively held. God put the desire within us.

A socio-economic issue we discussed in this book dealt with having both public and private enterprises functioning in a complementary fashion to meet the needs of society. Some people may question the practicality for having both public and private enterprises on equal footing within a social structure, whether the society entails the entire world or consists of a collection of nations as it does now. Indeed, why should a country have two socio-economic systems operating side-by-side?

A country could operate under a single system, provided all the important societal needs are met in an efficient and productive manner. However, a majority of nations in the world have found that some form of dual system works better. We know that many western nations, based on a free-enterprise or capitalistic economic system, are dominated by privately-owned businesses and enterprises. We also know they contain a large contingent of government–based social programs to meet their needs. To support a nation's citizenry, this includes public assistance, low-income housing, welfare, and food stamps. It includes unemployment insurance, disability insurance, subsidized home mortgages, and low interest college loans. It further includes child day care credit, public education for elementary and high school children, as well as assisted living entitlements and medical subsidies, like Medicare and Medicaid programs, for the elderly.

We should mention that none of these personal benefits ought to be provided "free"; that is, without any contribution from the people who receive them. Whether it's monetary as secured through taxation, or a product or service that's gained from actual employment, the recipients must contribute. For government to provide specific amenities and services without cost to the beneficiaries, in effect encourages a social-economic dependency that's counter productive in design. It degrades the social value of self-reliance, which is important to a person's feeling of self-worth.

For businesses and industries, some of the amenities government offers include low interest rate loans, low tax rates, and capital improvement subsidies. Additionally, there are incentives provided to corporations relative to employment practices that center on hiring quotas, guaranteed medical protection, standards on workplace safety, and so forth. Regardless of whether the government subsidies are designed to assist individual citizens or businesses and corporations, the list goes on and on.

For nations functioning under a totalitarian system, the government owns and operates the major industrial and commercial enterprises. It also controls national conglomerations that deal with communication and transportation, as well as power and energy. Similarly, the government determines the distribution of basic and supplemental benefits to its citizens, a distribution that's often based on political and ideological priorities. Although the businesses and industries in a totalitarian state may be privately owned, their operations are normally under the strict monitoring of government.

Neither the free-enterprise nor totalitarian system, by itself, has solved the economic needs of society in a completely satisfactorily manner. Each has shortcomings. In actual practice, neither private nor public-ownership affords total equality relative to the opportunity to be employed and attain the necessities of life and other amenities that are based on one's efforts and hard work.

A socio-economic system then must be fair to all participants. This means no individual and no business or industry, publicly or privately-owned, would be required to provide more support or bear a greater financial burden than others based upon their comparative levels of involvement. It would be true for any of the universal institutions of society that a person, business, or industry participates in.

Let's look at the employment world as it pertains to the contributions expected from and the rewards available to a person who participates in the universal institution design vs. a private enterprise system. As pointed out in chapter 6, individual citizens can participate in the universal institution of employment on a voluntary basis. Like businesses and industries, the private citizens can be involved at any level they wish. They can participate on a full or part-time basis in other institutions as well, such as education, health care, transportation, communication, and so forth, as part of a contributive effort towards the improvement of social living.

If individuals, businesses, or industries belong to the universal institution of employment on a full-time basis they will be compensated for their work. That is, they will receive pay, products, and services based on their accomplishments. If they work part-time in the universal institution of employment, they will receive credit towards the products and services they wish to use. The level of credit, in the form of vouchers, will be in proportion to the level of involvement, or work, they perform in the employment institution. If the individuals, businesses, or industries don't participate in the universal institution of employment, they will have to pay for any products or services that are generated by the several universal institutions of society. Hence, if you work exclusively in the private sector, you will have to pay to use any facility or receive any service that's provided in the public sector.

Thereby, a citizen can participate in any universal institution or private sector enterprise to whatever extent he or she wishes by paying for the service be it in transportation, communication, energy, education, utility-services, etc. For example, if you used a major public highway you will pay a toll. If you needed medical treatment at a universal (public) health care clinic, you will be charged a fee for the services rendered. For all citizens, whether privately or publicly employed, the cost would be appropriately adjusted to be fair and equitable.

In the socio-economic system we propose, a nation's manufactured products and most of its needed services would not be the responsibility of the government. Instead, they would be provided by the universal institution of employment, wherein everyone who's able to work must work to receive the benefits of societal life. Only those individuals who are physically or mentally incapable of supporting themselves would be taken care of by the employment institution. The source of support for other able-bodied people, who are unwilling to work, might come from members within their respective families, charitable organizations, or the church.

In chapter 5, we outlined a design for a universal institution of government wherein the emphasis for choosing representatives to a nation's congress should be based on the following criteria. We said the representatives ought to be selected because of their support for either individual rights and liberties, or the rights of the general public and society at large. It's important to note this delineation isn't intended to highlight potential conflicts between the private enterprise sector and the universal institutions of society. We don't want these two systems to be competitive nor confrontational. Rather, the goal is to have both the private and public-based systems co-exist on equal footing. In actual practice, no doubt the public sector would be comprised of a significant percentage of privately-owned businesses and industries that participate on a voluntary basis.

Government resides in the public sector of society. Indeed, all the universal institutions are in the public sector. They provide services across the broad spectrum of society for all of its citizens.

We note that a universal government institution only owns and operates those entities which fall under its immediate jurisdiction such as the law enforcement facilities, prisons, court houses, military bases, and parklands. It wouldn't own or operate public school systems, community hospitals, or the nation's highway system. These responsibilities belong to their respective institutions of education, health care, and transportation. A key role of government in regards to public-based enterprises, which reside in other institutions, is to raise revenues whenever necessary through taxation and then distribute the revenues to the appropriate institutions. This assumes that the other institutions don't acquire all of their needed resources through the fees they charge and the incomes they receive from the products they sell or services they render.

The universal institution of government, specifically the legislative and executive branches, will partner with the managing boards of the several institutions of society to raise sufficient revenues to maintain the institutions. The board of ministers of the executive branch and the managerial boards of the universal institutions will work in unison to ensure the financial resources are available. For the most part, each institution will raise its own funds through the products it generates and the services it performs. Should an institution be unable to raise the necessary income, it's the government's duty to provide additional resources through taxation and other fees. It's likely there will be a tax designated for each major institution of society. For example, government would levy separate taxes to support education, health care, recreation, communication, transportation, environment, and so forth. The revenues will be forwarded to the appropriate institutions to meet operating expenses as determined by the institutions' boards of managers.

Since the institution of employment is involved in meeting the subsistence needs of food, clothing, and shelter, it should be able to raise most, if not all, of the operating funds it requires through the sale of building supplies, wearing apparel, and food products. Therefore, it's probable that government wouldn't have to provide financial support to the institution of employment. Likewise, based on the concept of separation of church and state, the institution of religion would raise its own funds and not receive any governmental assistance. And since the institution of family consists of individual households, each involved in its personal endeavors, nearly all the needs of families, financial or otherwise, would be met via their participation in employment and other social venues.

Another area where there's a sharing of responsibility between the universal institution of government and societal institutions is in the process of setting safety standards. This involves construction and building codes. It involves codes on clothing apparel as well as requirements regarding the nutritional content of foods. It applies to reliability standards on manufactured products and safety regulations in the workplace. It also applies to standards in education relative to curriculums, achievement tests, graduation requirements, etc. Guidelines on the proper use of medicines, as well as environmental requirements regarding the monitoring of pollutants, toxins, etc., are included. It further involves setting up procedures on the performance of general service jobs.

Each of the major institutions of society determines procedures for internal operations, and each establishes principles by which it conducts day-to-day business. Likewise, each establishes standards to comply with the safety requirements that are drafted into law by the legislative branch of government. Once the standards are established, it is government's responsibility to ensure they are fair and enforced.

A similar operational alignment occurs between government and the various institutions on issues dealing with the response to national emergencies such as forest fires, earthquakes, floods, etc. The main responsibility lies with the executive branch of government, which provides the personnel, equipment, and financial resources. The personnel include emergency responders and medical technicians, as well as firefighters, and security officers. During such times, the executive branch can also activate a national guard.

The managerial boards of the various institutions set up the protocols for response to emergency situations which occur within their respective fields of operation. Depending on the seriousness of the emergency, its locale, and the number of citizens being affected, the institutions work side-by-side with the institution of government to resolve the crises.

In regard to the pros and cons of publicly and privately-based economic systems, the bottom line for living under either system is that every able-bodied person has to work in order to earn the benefits and rewards. Likewise, everyone is accountable for his or her actions in a social environment. Hence, the basis for government to enact laws and make decisions dealing with individual vs. public rights is to ensure that every citizen has equal access to legal proceedings, wherein the outcome of those proceedings is founded on equality and justice. Without question, the public's interest is important to the well-being of society as a whole. In this regard, it is government's duty to make sure all citizens are protected from infringement by self-serving entities which would harm the stability of society and its several institutions.

The role of government then isn't to own or dominate a major institution of society. The institutions of employment, education, health care, transportation, communication ought to function on their own merits. As pointed out, they would be administered by their respective board of elected managers. Government's role is to make sure these institutions are managed with a sense of fairness to their employees and the citizens they serve. It's government's role to ensure the various institutions have the freedom to carry out their own areas of responsibilities in a just manner.

As discussed previously, a universal institution of society, be it education, health care, etc., will be successful as long as the employment structure promotes a work environment whereby people can work at occupations that advance the culture of man. It's a work environment where one attains the necessities of life for himself and his family, gains a sense of accomplishment and self-fulfillment, and provides care for those individuals who are unable to take care of themselves.

We should note that an individual employed in the universal institution of health, education, or recreation, as well as in any of the requisite institutions of transportation, communication, energy, utilities-services, etc., is working to improve the overall quality of life. One would be entitled to the same necessities, amenities, credits, etc. as a person who is working in the universal institution of employment, which focuses on providing the basic necessities of food, clothing, and housing to the citizens.

Earlier we wondered why a nation would function better under a hybrid social-economic system rather than under a public or private system alone. The answer is both publicly and privately-based employment structures are valuable to society. The advantage of a publicly-based, universal employment structure is that it provides the opportunity to all members of society to participate and achieve their purpose in life. That purpose is to advance the overall quality of human life and become the gardener and governor of Nature. A full description of man's purpose in life is presented in the book, *A Pen Named Man: Our Purpose*. It is equally important that the private ownership employment structure be kept intact. People who work in the private sector realm must also have the opportunity to pursue their occupations and fulfill their purpose in life.

Both a private and a public-based employment structure can co-exist, and in regard to equality and fairness, it's appropriate they do so. Every person should have the freedom to pursue his or her dreams to operate an enterprise that's of value to society. Just as every person has a right to choose an occupation that suits one's interests, he or she has the right to own a company that provides gainful employment to others. And just as everyone has a right to live where he or she wants, purchase the necessities of life and amenities he or she desires, and pursue the recreation endeavors he or she enjoys, so every person has a right to buy and sell property, secure copyrights and patents, and start up his or her own business, etc. Furthermore, just as a person has a right to run for elected office and serve in government, so one has the right to be an entrepreneur within the business world.

Hence, as with many aspects of social life, the satisfaction an individual gains from creating a new business is commendable, and it can serve as the avenue for pursuing one's purpose in life. Finally, we might add that like every other citizen, the owner of a business can participate to whatever extent he desires, either individually or through his enterprise, in the various universal institutions of society.

It's of interest to speculate on how societies of the future might be structured. If we consider civic and social functions being aligned according to their respective institutions, we can project a design which illustrates how an urban center of tomorrow might be fashioned. For example, a metropolitan area could be built in concentric circular fashion, with the city streets extending out from a hub. From an overhead view, it might look like the trunk of a tree with its numerous rings of annual growth. Other designs could have the same format, but rather than being concentric circles, the layout of the streets might be in other geometric patterns such as a square, rectangle, or octagon.

The city's hub, or center, would be home to the local government, containing its legislative, executive, and judicial office buildings. The first circle out from the hub would contain the main operational centers for the several institutions of society. Located in this city "block" would be the administrative offices for the education, health care, transportation, communication, energy, utilities-services, and so forth. The next area of the metropolitan design could contain several blocks dedicated to the institution of employment. These circles of streets would contain the businesses and industries where citizens work to manufacture the products that are consumed by society. The next couple of blocks could contain churches, mosques, and synagogues as well as the educational and charitable facilities that belong to the institution of religion. The next grouping of streets could house the shopping malls, retail stores, and restaurants. The next of the level of circular streets would house the educational, health care, and recreational facilities of society. This grouping of streets would contain schools and universities; medical facilities such as doctor offices, clinics, and hospitals; and entertainment venues including theaters, indoor gymnasiums, sports stadiums, outdoor fields for soccer, football, baseball, etc. Next could come several blocks of residential streets, which contain single and multiple family dwellings, apartment buildings, hotels, etc.

Depending upon the size of the municipality, there would be a repeating pattern to designated areas which extend outwardly from the city's center. Mimicking the initial format, the concentric regions would contain business and industry, houses of worship, retail outlets, educational and health care units, recreational facilities, and expanded sections of residential homes. Obviously, the size of a city and its designated areas would vary. There could be smaller cities with just a single circle of each major sector of society, such as one area for schools and hospitals. Conversely, there could be very large metropolitan area that has repetitive concentric circles throughout its structure, including three or four separate areas for schools, hospitals, etc.

The proposed metropolitan design would preferably contain high speed subway and monorail systems with terminals located at the outermost regions and extending from there in a straight line, similar to spokes in a wheel, into the hub of the city. Similar routes would be connected to these lines at major intersections, and thereby the systems would transverse the city in circular fashion, sector by sector. Certain subways lines would be dedicated to the manufacturing sector and carry raw materials, intermediate components, and merchandise into the city. These lines would likewise transport manufactured goods and products out from the city to designated shipping terminals. Other faster moving monorail lines would move people in typical passenger car fashion, into work areas, educational and health care facilities, shopping centers, government offices, etc. People would use the monorail lines for the purposes of going to work, shopping, attending church, and conducting personal business.

Lastly, the subway and monorail networks wouldn't be the only means of travel within the metropolitan areas. Like the highway systems of today, the city streets would be laid out with intersections in a crisscrossing fashion and fully utilized by automobile, bus, and truck traffic.

It's of interest to take note of the functional relationships which exist among the major institutions of society. Based on their roles in society, we can identify two types of universal institutions. One type can be labeled as "stand-alone" and includes the institutions of family, religion, and government. These institutions are able to perform independently when it comes to meeting their societal responsibilities. For example, the institution of family involves the personal behavior aspects of life. Family entails a common set of values that are based on interpersonal relationships, as defined via the input of biologically related people living together in an emotionally secure environment. Likewise, the institution of religion exists as a moral compass on human behavior. It directly ties man's temporal life and his feelings of worth to the eternal presence of a divine creator. Further, the institution of government is involved with aspects of social life that pursues a quest for law and order. Government focuses on upholding the rights of citizens, which are based on a sense of fairness and equality.

We should mention these institutions can carry out their duties independently, but they don't stand alone per se. For sure, they are interconnected and interrelated to the other institutions in regard to maintaining a stable social environment. As a matter of fact, the traditional institution of religion doesn't stand alone when it's in a position to manage the political and socio-economic forces of society as in the case of a theocracy. Similarly, the institution of modern-day government doesn't stand alone when it's able to control all or most of a nation's industrial, commercial, communication, and energy enterprises as in the case of a monarchy or totalitarian state. Nonetheless, religion and government have unique responsibilities separate from the socio-economic sphere. We're well aware that religion's importance lies in tying temporal human existence to an eternal deity. And government, as a defining universal institution of society, has a special role in serving as the guardian of the other institutions of society. And finally, the institution of family definitely does stand alone.

The other type of universal institution can be identified as "non-stand alone". The non-stand alone ones include the universal institution of basic necessities, otherwise known as employment; the supplemental institutions of education, health care, and recreation; and the requisite institutions of communication, transportation, energy, etc. These institutions act independently, yet they support one another in providing the materials, technologies, processes, and products to move a nation forward. The non-stand alone institutions collectively form the socio-economic fabric of society. The means to earning a decent living and interacting successfully with one's fellow citizens are founded in the collaborative efforts of these several institutions.

Let's now look at the path forward relative to human cultural development. In general, our patterns of behavior are notably molded by the social orders to which we ascribe. We establish social values which help us define proper behavior; and a social value of significance involves our interpersonal relationships and how we relate to one another. Indeed, we must promote communication and cooperation as we engage our fellow citizens in everyday events. As we expand the avenues of human interaction in positive and supportive ways, we'll be in a better position to advance the cultural achievements of man.

It's worthwhile to reiterate why mankind ought to establish a universal social-economic employment structure. First of all, the people who participate will be guaranteed the basic necessities of life throughout their lifetime. We've already identified these as a housing allotment, food, and clothing. Secondly, the people who participate will be guaranteed the supplemental necessities which include unlimited medical care, a well-rounded education, and access to public recreational facilities. Thirdly, the social-economic system will afford people, who are unable to work because of physical or mental health limitations, the same benefits that are awarded to people who work and participate. Fourthly, the successful operation of the social-economic system will provide a number of career development amenities. These amenities include the opportunity for everyone to work in an occupation of one's interests, skills set, and choosing. Additional job-related benefits include fairness in hiring, unbiased opportunity for promotion, equitable pay, job security, etc. Overall, a newly designed system should lead to a better working environment plus a higher standard of living for everyone involved. Finally, the successful operation of the social-economic system will facilitate man's attempt to achieve a key goal in life, which is to become the gardener and governor of Nature.

Across the world then, every person ought to be employed in an occupation that manufactures a product or provides a service useful to society. On a personal level, everyone needs to be employed in order to secure the basic necessities of life. And on the global scale, everyone must to be assured that his or her participation in a job will benefit the well-being of mankind.

A final thought. It may take mankind 1,000 years or 500,000 years to achieve the societal goals we've laid out. However, the timeline doesn't matter as much as the path. It's more important we continue to work towards improving the welfare of the human race, as well as other species of life, in whatever ways we can. As human culture unfolds, we'll be riding this carousel called Earth and going about our daily activities in the attempt to live good and decent lives.

Bibliography

Bourke, V. J. *Ethics.* New York: MacMillan, 1967.
Broom, L. and P. Selznick. *Sociology.* New York: Harper & Row, 1968.
Coleman, J. C. *Psychology & Effective Behavior.* Glenview, IL.: Scott, Foresman & Company, 1969.
DiVesta, F. J. and G. G. Thompson. *Educational Psychology.* New York: Appleton-Century-Crofts, 1970.
Easton, S. C. *The Western Heritage.* New York: Holt, Rinehart and Winston, 1961.
Fischer K. W. and A. Lazerson. *Psychology Today: an Introduction,* 2nd ed. Del Mar, CA: Communications, Research, Machines, 1972.
Gouldner, A. W. and H. P. Gouldner. *Modern Sociology.* New York: Harcourt, Brace & World, 1963.
Jones, W. T. et al. *Approaches to Ethics.* New York: McGraw-Hill, 1969.
Kagen, J. and E. Havemann. *Psychology, an Introduction.* New York: Harcourt Brace & World, 1968.
Kaplan, L. *Foundations of Human Behavior.* New York: Harper & Row, 1965.
Lindgren, H. C. and D. Byrne. *Psychology, An Introduction to a Behavioral Science.* New York: Wiley, 1971.
Moody, P. *Introduction to Evolution,* 2nd ed. New York: Harper & Brothers, 1962.
Morgan, C. T. *Introduction to Psychology.* New York: McGraw-Hill, 1961.
Noss, J. B. *Man's Religion,* 3rd ed. New York: MacMillan, 1963.
Rogers, J. S. et al. *Man and the Biological World.* New York: McGraw-Hill, 1952.
Samuelson, P. A. *Economics, An Introductory Analysis.* New York: McGraw-Hill, 1967.
Sprague, E. and P.W. Taylor. *Knowledge and Value.* New York: Harcourt, Brace & World, 1959.
Titus, H. and M. Keeton. *Ethics for Today.* New York: D. Van Nostrand, 1973.
The Holy Bible, King James Version. New York: Collins' Clear-Type Press, 1959.
The New Encyclopedia Britannica, 15th ed. Chicago: Encyclopedia Britannica, 2005.
The World Book Encyclopedia. Chicago: World Book, 2005
Villee, C. A. *Biology, The Human Approach.* Philadelphia: W.B. Saunders, 1950.
Wheelwright, P. *A Critical Introduction to Ethics.* New York: The Odyssey Press, 1959.

www.ingramcontent.com/pod-product-compliance
Lightning Source LLC
Chambersburg PA
CBHW050804160426
43192CB00010B/1636